Mill Memories

Interviews with Former Employees of Paisley's Thread Mills

Ferguslie Mill lassies 'cleekin' arms as they come through the gates at
the end of a shift (1950s)
Photo courtesy of Paisley Museum

Printed by
Greenlaw Graphics, Paisley

Foreword

A lot has been written - and rightly so - about the Clarks and Coats, the families who came from ordinary beginnings to turn Paisley into a world-famous thread town during the 19th and 20th centuries. But the thousands of men and women who worked in the Anchor and Ferguslie mills have not received the recognition they deserve. As one contributor remarked in an aside, the sweat of the mill workers built the magnificent Coats Memorial Church and made the Clark and Coats families wealthy.

This book is a celebration of these Paisley mill workers. Many have moved to other parts of the world and many have become involved with other areas of work, but even so, they have never forgotten their mill days and are still in close contact with the friends they made there. As another contributor said, 'In those days, Paisley was the mills, and the mills were Paisley.'

The three final interviews are with people who were not directly employed in the mills, but contributed in other ways to the progress of the Paisley area's proud textile history.

My thanks go to Catherine McNally and June Quail, who gathered names and also did some of the interviewing, to Sadie Turnbull, who helped with the photographs, and to Eleanor Clark for permission to use the booklet she wrote at the time of the mills' 150th anniversary as the source of the brief history on the mill owners.

My thanks also go to those men and women who agreed to be interviewed for this book. It was a pleasure and a privilege to meet each and every one of them.

Evelyn Hood

These elegant and well-dressed Edwardian ladies, with their immaculate hairstyles, were Paisley mill girls, possibly 'toe typists' from Ferguslie Mills' Twisting Department (note the bare feet and tools of their trade - scissors, left and right back row & front row right, and the loop of twine attached to the belt of the girl centre, back row).

Photo Courtesy of the Old Paisley Society.

Paisley's Thread Mill Families

Paisley's two great thread mills owed their existence to men born of humble stock. **James Coats**, the son of a weaver, was born in 1774 in a small thatched cottage at 4 Northcroft, Paisley. After taking up his father's trade, he spent six years in the Ayrshire Fencibles in the South of England. On his discharge he returned to Paisley on foot to resume his trade. From weaving he moved to the tambouring trade and then to manufacturing canton crepe shawls, eventually going into thread manufacture.

In the late 18th century the brothers **Peter and James Clark** were working as weavers' furnishers in Paisley. When the weaving business was hit by Napoleon's Berlin Decree banning exports to Great Britain around 1806, **Peter Clark** was prompted to experiment in producing heddles of cotton instead of silk. The Clark family then began manufacturing cotton thread on part of the Anchor Mills site in 1812.

Fourteen years later, at the other end of the town, **James Coats** built a small thread-making factory at Ferguslie.

James Clark, born in a thatched cottage, at 10 Cotton Street, Paisley in 1782, had worked as a young boy on making heddles for weavers, along with his brothers **William and Andrew,** and **Alexander Wilson**, who was to become the famous ornithologist. From these humble beginnings, **James**, along with his brother **John**, became chiefly responsible for developing the thread industry founded by their father.

In 1830 **James and Peter Coats** took over the Ferguslie factory from their father, paying him a rent of £500 per annum. By 1840 hard work had increased the trade of the firm and the size of the factory. Three quarters of the Coats' product went to America at this time

As both companies, the Clarks and the Coats, thrived there was great rivalry between them in the U.S.A. as well as in Paisley. However, in 1896 **Clark & Co.** and **J. & P. Coats Limited** amalgamated under the Coats name, and later that year they were joined by Brook Brothers of Meltharn and James Chadwick & Brother of Bolton.

Despite the amalgamation both companies retained their distinctive trademarks, and the Paisley people have always referred to the two great mill complexes as 'Clarks' and 'Coats.'

From the earliest, working conditions were of a high standard in both Anchor and Ferguslie Mills, with up-to-date facilities for the time. Working hours compared well with other industries, and employees enjoyed such facilities as canteens, which date from the 1880's, hot baths, dwelling houses, hostels for girls and medical and fire services.

Long service was acknowledged from the late 19th century and in 1920 a pension scheme was introduced.

Great interest was taken in education and one of the most obvious examples is the Half Timers' School, which was built at Ferguslie in 1887.

Both the Coats and Clark families have been responsible for many donations and gifts to the town of Paisley, and indeed elsewhere.

Source 'Coats the Threadmakers, 1830-1980' by Eleanor Clark, a booklet written at the time of the 150th Anniversary Exhibition in the Museum and Art Galleries, Paisley.

Listed Contents in Order

The magnificent Half Timers' School built at Ferguslie Mills by Coats in the 19th century for their youngest workers. The youngsters spent half their day in school and the other half working at their machines.

Photo Courtesy of Old Paisley Society

Memories from Wards 1 and 4 of Hawkhead Hospital, Paisley

Jobs may come and jobs may go, but for some reason that casual phrase doesn't seem to include former Paisley thread mill workers. For them, the saying should be, 'Once a mill worker, always a mill worker.' Or so it seems in the town's Hawkhead Hospital, where many former mill lassies now live.

When they get together in the wards, their favourite topic of conversation is the time they worked in Anchor or Ferguslie Mills. Here are some of their memories.

Annie (Thomson) Kelly went into the mills in 1927, when she was 14 years old. 'In those days you gave your pay packet to your mother, unopened, because she needed the money. And you got a shilling a week for pocket money.'

Like most of the mill workers, **Jean (Buchanan) Hosie** went there straight from school. 'I started work in the Spooling Flat at Ferguslie Mills in 1925, then moved to the Anchor Mills when Ferguslie closed down. I was a mill worker for 46 years, always in Spooling.'

A Notion for Bowling

Jean started off as a runner for the piece-workers, then a bogie-girl, taking the bogies, or trollies, filled with completed reels of thread off to their next destination. Then she became a Weilds spinner. 'We needed to keep our scissors handy to cut the thread, and I mind that I kept my scissors hanging from my little finger. It was almost worn away!'

Two of Jean's sisters worked in the mill, and her mother had a small shop in Castle Street. 'It was opposite Cross Street - a general a 'things shop.' Jean joined the mill dressmaking class and learned how to make her own clothes, but the one thing she had always had a notion to try - bowling - seemed out of her reach because Ferguslie Mills Bowling Club was for male staff only.

'One day I was over seeing the mill chiropodist, and I mentioned to him that I would have liked to be a bowler. He suggested that I should join the Anchor Bowling Club, which did allow women. I thought that only Anchor workers could be in that club, but it turned out that I was wrong. By the time I left the chiropodist's room I had an application form for the Anchor Mill Bowling Club.'

The Ferguslie Mills Club's loss was Anchor Mills gain, for Jean was accepted into the Anchor club and went on to become a championship player. She loved the sport, and played right up until she was 80 years of age.

Always Pleased to get Back

'I loved working in the mills. I even missed my work during our annual two weeks' holidays. Don't get me wrong, I had a very happy family life, but I was always pleased to get back to the mill after the holidays. I made a lot of friends there, like Ellen Connell and Kitty Marshall, and never lost them.'

Most mill girls were very keen on dancing, but Jean was not alone in her passion for bowling. **Bessie Henderson** and **Ruby Brown**, both residents of Hawkhead Hospital, were enthusiastic bowlers, and Ruby, who at one time was Mistress of the department where Jean worked, was still bowling at the age of ninety. Her daughters have inherited her love of the sport, and through them Ruby, a Past President of Priorscroft Bowling Club in Paisley, has been able to keep in touch with bowling news.

Ruby, born in 1899, was a twiner and one of the young women sent abroad to teach local workers in the mills Coats set up in various countries. In Ruby's case, it was America.

'Oh, my mother cried and cried when I went. She kept saying that I was too young to go so far away. I cried myself, because I was homesick at first, but once I got over that I loved it. The folk there were that good to us, and you get awful confident when you travel. I think that the mill owners in Paisley did very well by their workers, I've got no complaints about that.'

Not everyone enjoyed their time in the mills. **May Boyce**, who also went into the Twining Department at Ferguslie Mills, only stuck it for a year before leaving. 'I hated it. I hated everything about it, and after a year I left to become a nurse.'

'You just had to like it, you didn't have any other option,' said **Nellie (Young) Campbell**, who spent two years in Rewinding at Ferguslie Mill. 'When I left school, everyone worked in the mills, and my mother made me go there too.'

Many of the former mill girls say, when asked why they chose the mills, 'My mother needed the money I could earn.' A considerable number of them were the main wage earners in their families, and once they achieved the grand old age of 16, the wages were good.

'There Was the Pension!'

The other general comment is, 'There was the pension!' Paisley mill girls were among the first to get a pension, which, with the reasonable salaries - which they worked hard to earn - gave them an independence that not every woman in the early-to-mid-20th century was able to enjoy. 'You were somebody if you were a mill girl,' said Ruby Brown. 'I got on well with the bosses, and never had a bad boss.'

'I liked it,' agreed **Ellen Herries**, who also worked in Ferguslie, guide cutting in the Spooling Department, while Bessie Henderson, who worked in No 8 Mill at Ferguslie, says, 'I loved my work.' Bessie was another keen bowler.

The general feeling among the former mills workers now living in Hawkhead Hospital, was that folk got on well with each other in the mills. 'Probably because there wasn't any envy,' said one. 'In those days you accepted your life and got on with it and didn't waste time wanting to have more or to be someone else.'

In the first half of the 20th century the twiners, operating the big twisting machines, had to work in their bare feet because they used their big toes to switch the machines on and off. **Ann Fairful**, who lived some distance from Ferguslie Mill and used to walk the three miles to work and three miles back home for every shift, remembers that the twiners referred to themselves as 'big toe typists'. 'Working with bare feet was nice and cool, and the lanolin in the yarn kept the skin nice.'

But some of the workers paid in later life when they developed trouble in their overworked big toes, and several had to undergo amputation. One resident had an aunt who, after years of working in a department where the air was filled with 'ouse' - tiny flecks of cotton which covered the workers' hair and clothes - had eventually to have an operation to remove a wad of cotton from her throat. 'She had a big scar across the base of her neck for the rest of her life.'

'Full Go Ahead'

Annie Kelly worked at the cotton mill (Ferguslie) before moving to the Anchor Embroidery Mill. 'When I was working at Ferguslie I remember getting out of bed early to catch the 7 o'clock mill bus. We had to be in our places at 7.30 waiting for the wee red light that told us to start work. Then it was a case of "full go ahead." Some of the frames were ready to be "doffed" - removing the full bobbins. It was very warm, and we took our shoes and stockings off and worked in our bare feet, which was cooler.

'It was a happy place to work, I remember the women singing at their machines. In the Anchor Mill I was a repairer, throwing out the bad work and repairing what we could. I was a great one for falling over boxes and things, and I mind once when I got the job of taking round filled rolls for the workers' tea break, I tripped right in front of the foreman's desk, and the rolls went flying everywhere. It was embarrassing, but at the same time, it was very funny.'

Nan (Stewart) Dickie, another resident, never actually worked in the mills but her father, David Stewart, worked in Coats' Central Agency in Glasgow. The family had one of the smart mill houses in

Thistle Street, near the Ferguslie Mills Cricket Club ground 'In those days,' says Nan, who kept house for her father and her two brothers, 'only the front row looking onto Corsebar Road had inside toilets. There were three rows of houses, all later upgraded.'

There were fond memories of the Mill Outings by charabanc, bus and train. Favourite places included Saltcoats, Largs, Portobello and Braemar, and one of **Jean Hosie's** favourite memories was a weekend trip to London for some of the mill workers.

During working hours, the toilets were the centre of the mill girls' social lives. There, they snatched the odd five minutes, perhaps managing to stretch it into ten minutes, to have a quick gossip, get their hair curled for the evening's dancing, have their nails done, 'there was always someone good at filing and polishing your nails for you,' and even learn dancing and crocheting.

'Where's Annie Kelly?'

'I remember getting my hair put into rollers in the toilets,' said Annie Kelly. 'The foreman, Adrian Houston, would be outside shouting, "Where's Annie Kelly?" and I would go out with my hair in rollers. He always knew where to find me on a Friday.'

The main activity that went on in the toilets, and the one they all remember fondly, was ear piercing. Sometimes it was done with a potato behind the ear, sometimes with an ordinary rubber, sometimes with a cake of soap, but the deed was always done with a big darning needle. In the very early days, twine was used to keep the holes open until healed, but later they got proper sleepers.

'What did you freeze the lobes with first?' asked a young nurse when she heard the residents discussing those ear-piercing sessions. 'Ice cubes?'

'What? No!' she was told. 'We didn't need anything but a potato or a cake of soap, and the darning needle.'

Didn't it hurt? 'Not really, but there were some lassies got infected, and had awful sore ears.'

Elizabeth Smith, a nurse at Hawkhead Hospital, who was herself a mill worker in the Anchor Mills from 1956 until 1959, says nostalgically, 'I wish I had a penny now for every set of ears I pierced in the Mill toilets.' Elizabeth used a cake of soap for the purpose. She was a desk girl in the Finishing Department, and loved the work. 'The money was better than you would have earned in an office. And the hen nights were great.' Her own hen night consisted of tea in the La Scala Picture House restaurant, followed by a film.

'I got the usual treatment on my last day at work before I got married - they covered my coat in tissue paper and took me through the streets with the usual chanty filled with salt and various wee dolls in it. Then they put me on a bus and left me to go home on my own with no money for the fare. I had to get off at the next stop and walk home. But it was all good clean fun, no harm in it.'

The sociable mill lassies always enjoyed a good night out. Often, in the 1950s and 1960's, they were held in someone's home..
Photo Courtesy of Old Paisley Society

The Ménage

Then there was the ménage. One worker undertook to collect a small sum - sixpence, a shilling, or perhaps two shillings - from her colleagues every Friday pay day, and keep it safe until Christmas, or the Fair Holidays, when it would be given back in lump sums. Several people recalled one occasion when the collector absconded with the money just before it was due to be paid out, and the disappointed girls had to go home and tell their mothers that their months of saving had resulted in no extra spending money at all.

But that is all part of life's rich tapestry, and like everything else, it was accepted and the world kept turning. After all, as every one of the former mill workers now living in Hawkhead Hospital demonstrates, Paisley folk are survivors. And Paisley mill workers were special. Very special indeed.

Paisley owes a great debt to them.

Nan (Hooper) Owen

Nan Hooper was heartbroken when in April 1919 she had to leave school at the age of 13. Her father, badly injured during the First World War, was a patient in Stobhill Hospital and the family needed Nan's wage.

Her father was so angry at the thought of his daughter having to cut her education short that when he was able, he went to the School Board to ask if she could return to school. Unfortunately it was too late, as she had been out of school for six months.

Miss Morrison, one of Nan's teachers at Williamsburgh School, tried through her own father, a manager at McDowall's Starchworks, to find a job there for her, but unfortunately the starchworks only paid girls 12/- (60 pence) a week, while the Anchor Mills paid 19/-. (95 pence)

Desperate to see her daughter in employment, Nan's mother went with her to the Anchor Mill gatehouse to ask if the girl could get a job. Her gamble paid off, for the gatekeeper, Mr McClatchie, passed mother and daughter over to one of the managers, Mr Crawford.

'She's Good at Embroidery'

When he asked Nan's mother what sort of job she wanted for her daughter she said, 'Anything but licking tickets and working with her bare feet (in the Twining Department the machinery was operated by the workers' big toes) but she's good at embroidery.'

Nan was taken on to work in the Box Shop as a bender, shaping cardboard boxes. A diligent worker, she is still proud to recall that by the time she was 18 years old she had become fully qualified in her job. She worked so fast that during her training one fellow worker openly doubted the quality of her work. Mr Tulloch, Nan's department manager at the time, set up a test and Nan was proved to be a superb worker, both in speed and quality.

In order to get her School Leaving Certificate, Nan began to attend night-school classes at Paisley Grammar School, studying Arithmetic, English and Grammar and paying 2/6d. (12 and a half pence) per term. Later, having maintained perfect attendance, she went on to study Modern Science and Good Housekeeping. Nan still wears the gold ring her father gave her when she completed her studies.

As a result of her studies there was talk of moving Nan to the Embroidery Mill, but as that would have meant a drop in wages she stayed where she was. When she reached her 18th birthday Nan went onto piecework. One of her closest friends in the mill was Jessie McAteer, who later moved in with Nan's family as a lodger, after her own father remarried.

Nan loved being in the mill, but her younger sister, who had followed her into the mill, hated her work in the Gassing Department. At 15 years of age she rebelled and announced that she would not go back to the mill. A quarrel blew up, and after her mother slapped her, Nan's sister ran away from home but later returned and settled down to work at Robertson's Factory.

A Royal Visit

One of Nan's mill memories concerns a visit by the then Prince of Wales. Nan recalls him as being nice-looking, though she was disappointed to discover that he was quite a small man, not as tall as she had expected. She also recalls that he wore make-up, and says that at one point she was close enough to him to smell it.

Nan left the mills when she married in 1927 but was asked back in 1935 when a lot of the male workers were joining the armed forces. She started back as a cleaner and was soon in charge of 18 women. She also worked in the paper mill in the afternoons.

One of her jobs was cleaning the Counting House, used by Oscar Clark and Sir Malcolm McDougall. Sir Malcolm used one of the rooms as a gun room and only Nan was allowed to clean in there. Her work was valued and when alterations were made in the layout of the Counting Office Mr Curr, a senior manager, asked for Nan's opinion in the matter and paid her £30 for her advice.

Nan stayed on with the mill for 30 years, until it closed down.

Catherine (Elliott) (McAuley) Burns

The oldest in her family, Cathy Ellliott started work in Anchor Mills one month before her 12th birthday. 'My father was blown up by a bomb in France during the Great War and my mother had to raise five children on her own. We lived in a kitchen in Andrew Street, then later we moved to Back Sneddon Street and eventually to Gordon Street. That was a lovely house, it had a bath. There wasn't much money but my mother always kept us clean and fed - I would have done anything for her.

'When I left the North School I went to work in the mill because it was the only job there was. I was started right away and put to sweeping floors for six weeks, then I was banged into piecework in the Balling Department and that was that - on piecework you never got lifting your head from your work. Very few people in the mills were time-workers; we were almost all on piecework. The managers were mostly English, and they were very strict. Everything was timed - even when you went to the lavatory you were timed to make sure you didn't spend too long away from your work.'

'The Whole Place Erupted'

In Balling, the women put bands printed with 'Anchor Mills' round balls of crochet thread then packed the thread in boxes, which had to be stamped. 'Everything had to be done just right, or we got it to do over again. The work was heavy and hard - it was all hard work in the mills.'

Cathy well remembers the day when a woman who worked beside her decided that there would be no harm in taking home two stained balls of thread instead of sending them back. 'She hid them up the leg of her knickers and the next thing we knew the whole place had erupted, with whistles blowing and everything. The manager had seen her and she was sacked on the spot.'

Cathy's sister Harriet worked in the Twisting Department. 'They had to switch the machines off and on with their big toes; I mind my sister being in agony with the pain in her toe because of having to do that.'

'My name was down to be a dyer.'

Cathy left the mill when she married, but returned to it during the Second World War, when a lot of the male workers were called up and women took their places. 'Someone came to my door and said my name was down to be a dyer. I started on the 6 until 2 shift on May 9th 1941 just when Clydebank was being bombed, and as I walked to work on that first morning I saw the bombs falling over Renfrew.'

In the dye works, men and women alike had to protect themselves against the acids in the dyes by wearing dungarees, clogs, masks, headgear and gloves. 'The Dyeing Department was a dismal place, all steamy, and the work was heavy, but believe it or not I was happy there because the men were a great bunch to be with. Most of them had been made exempt from the Services for one reason or another, and came back to the mills.'

Cathy eventually had to give the job up because of arthritis in her shoulders. Widowed in her 20s, with two daughters to raise, she married a man she met in the dye works.

During her time in the mill, where she also worked in the Gassing and Examining Departments, Cathy only remembers one good manager, Archie McKinley. 'If he asked you to do something he would say, "I know I can rely on you." We each secretly believed that Archie thought we were the best worker in the department - we didn't realise that he said that to all of us. He was great to work for.'

Looking back, the only good memories Cathy has of her mill days is the warmth and friendship among the workers themselves. 'The wages were poor and the work was very hard, but the women were so cheery. A girl called Lizzie Findlay, just the same age as me, started in the mills on the same day, and we were close friends till Lizzie died aged 60.

'There was a closeness among the workers that folk who might have considered themselves to be in better jobs never knew.'

 # Helen (McGovern) Haughey

In 1922, at the age of 14, Helen McGovern went straight from school to the Twisting Department of Coat's Ferguslie Mill.

'I had three younger brothers and as they would have to learn a trade when they left school, I had to get a job with good money. I hated the smell of the machine oil and the caddis (ouse) that stuck to my hair and clothes, and most of all I hated the constant loud noise of the machinery as it twisted the cotton fibre into skeins. But girls had no choice then. It was the paper mill or Coats' Mill.

'I was scared stiff of the big machines as they were driven by long belts overhead and if a belt broke you had to run for your life. Of course all that changed in later years. Nevertheless we had good times too. If our frames were running good we could sit up in the toilets in a room attached, where we had sing-a-longs.

'I got used to the mill. We had some happy times. I made a lot of good friends in those days. We worked in our bare feet as we had to stop the spindle on which the bobbins ran with our big toes if a thread broke.

Helen (McGovern) Haughey in the early 1930s, with her husband Joseph and their son, also Joseph.
Photo Courtesy of the Haughey family

Helen Haughey pictured in 2001 with son Gerard and (left to right) daughters Catherine, Evelyn, Pat, Helen, Frances and Anne.
Photo Courtesy of the Haughey family

The Cost of Being a 'Toe Typist'

'I once got a deep cut on my toe and although it healed, I still felt pain which never went away over the years until finally it was discovered I had a tumour of thirty years growth, which exactly fitted in with the time I had cut it.

'We were all keen on ballroom dancing. We learned the music the bands played and someone always had song sheets with all the words. It was the gay twenties era. The Charleston was the favourite dance, with figure waltzes too. My pals and I went to the dance halls three or four nights a week.'

Helen, who grew up in Linwood, married and left the mills to raise her family. In the late 1950s she and her husband emigrated to Australia, where she has enjoyed a happy life. But, she says, 'to all immigrants, the place they were born in, city, town or village, that's home.'

Taken from A Walk Down Memory Lane - My Story Looking Back by Helen McGovern Haughey, compiled and edited by Helen (Haughey) Mitchell.

 # Rena (Fordie) Shaw

Rena Fordie was educated at St Catherine's School and left in 1923, aged 14. 'Because I did well at school I got a place working in the Counting House. I liked it but because the pay was better in the mills I asked for a transfer and ended up in the Mile End Reeling Department.

'The work there was physically hard, and when things were quiet in the Reeling we were sent over to the Gassing Department to work. That was where the thread was run through a flame to burn off any frayed ends. I didn't like that job either. There were two smaller machines called box-reelers in Mile End flat and they were easier to work than the other machinery. The job was quite specific and not everyone was suited to it, but eventually I was given one of these reelers, and the work wasn't so bad then.'

Like most of the women she worked beside in the mills Rena had, and still has, a strong sense of humour and a passion for going to the dancing whenever she could find the time. 'Although you had to work hard for your wages there were quite a lot of young lassies round about my own age in the departments, and we had a lot of good times together. Anchor Mills had a Recreation Club and I remember playing tennis there. And we had Gala Days too.'

Rena (Fordie) Shaw, 2nd right, and her husband Charlie Shaw, a tenter, enjoying a day on the beach with friends. All the people in the picture worked in the Paisley mills.
Photo Courtesy of Rena Shaw

Bad Supervisors could Make Life a Misery

Looking back, Rena thinks that the worst job was probably in the Cotton Mill, where the machinists had to work in their bare feet. 'The air in there was thick with cotton and they were covered with it when they came out after a shift. A lot of them suffered later in life from chest problems.'

In the mills, with their strict rules, a difficult supervisor could make the workers' lives a misery. Rena recalls a friend in the Cotton Mill who was persistently ignored when she flapped her apron, a request in mill sign language for permission to go to the lavatory. In those days nobody was allowed to leave a machine without permission, and the poor woman eventually had to give up work because of chronic health problems.

'There was quite a division between the Ferguslie Mills and the Anchor Mills in my day. When I started going out with a lad who worked in Ferguslie Mills my mother disapproved. She wanted me to stick with my own kind - lads that worked at the Anchor Mills.'

Despite her mother's misgivings Rena married her Coats Mill sweetheart, Charlie Shaw, and left the mills after thirteen years there to raise her family.

 # Bill Peacock

Bill Peacock was just a week past his 14th birthday when, in 1927, he started work in the Ferguslie Mills dye works. 'We lived in Neilston Road - the Charleston district. They used to call it Kentucky. I went to the South School. In the mills I served my time as an apprentice in the dye works, attending night school at the Paisley Tech. I had a cousin, the same name as me, and exactly the same age - he went into the mill laboratory.'

After serving his time Bill learned colour matching, eventually becoming assistant to Jimmy Howe, the main colour matcher for the mills. 'When customers requested certain colours we had to find the perfect match or make up the shade specially. We had 354 standard shades and almost 4000 specials, as well as about 1000 shades used for a special order from an English mill. They were a great crowd in the dye works. Everyone had a nickname.'

Bandsman

Early on in his career Bill joined the Ferguslie Mills Brass and Reed Band. 'In the Boys' Brigade I had learned to play the trumpet and the cornet, the instrument I played most of the time, and I enjoyed every minute of my time as a band member. We used to practice in the dye works dining hall, then moved to a hall at Green Road, then to the Half Timers' School. We had an excellent bandmaster, Mr Caldwell; he was a foreman in the Spinning Mill. After his death our bandmaster was Mr Thomson, who didn't work in the mill himself. We played in all the Paisley parks, and sometimes in the summer we played in seaside towns, like Saltcoats.'

One of Bill's brothers was a sub-manager in the Spinning Mill, and another brother was the mill's glazier.

In 1940 Bill Peacock went into the RAF, and served until 1945. 'Music

Ferguslie Mills Brass and Reed Band Circa 1930s/40s.
Photo Courtesy of Bill Peacock

helped to take some of the weight of the war off my shoulders. I was never a member of the famous Squadronnaires, but I had the pleasure of playing with them on a few occasions.'

Playing before the King and Queen

The musical highlight of the war for Bill was being invited to take part in a duet played in Oxford before King George V1 and Queen Elizabeth. 'I'll never forget that occasion.'

When he returned to the mills after the war someone else had taken over his job, so he was given the position of foreman in the Hank-Winding Department on the south side. 'We hank-wound onto bobbins which we then despatched to the Polishing Department in the adjacent mill. The mills were connected by a passageway. It was all women in the Hank-Winding, most of them on piecework. Some of them were great ones for taking a rise out of you but it didn't worry me, I got on fine with them. Three of the older women taught the newcomers, and helped to keep an eye on the department. At that time we had quite a lot of women from Czechoslovakia in the mills, and we needed an interpreter, which caused some interesting moments.'

End of the Ferguslie Mills

Bill also returned to the mill band, taking over for a short time as bandmaster when Mr Thomson died. 'By then Ferguslie was in the process of closing down and the work was being transferred to the Anchor Mills, so I had the job of dispersing the instruments and sheet music and winding up the band. Music has been an important part of my life. I played with two orchestras and three bands, including the Johnstone and Renfrew Bands, where I helped out if they needed a player.'

He and his wife are also closely involved with their church (Victoria Place Baptist Church, now Central Baptist Church). They both sang in the choir - Bill was a choir member for 55 years as well as being senior deacon for a number of years. Although he has now given up singing he is actively involved with The Nightingales, a group including his wife who, under the guidance of musical director Alex McKinnon, himself a former mill employee, provide musical entertainment mainly for pensioners' clubs.

As Bill was just two years off retiring when the Hank-Winding Department closed down, he then left the mill.

Looking back, he says, 'I can't complain - I enjoyed my time in the mills.'

 # Margaret (Young) Blackie

Margaret Young started work in the Anchor Mills in the late 1920s, at the age of 14. 'I tried to get into the mills the week before my 14th birthday, but when they found out my true age they sent me home - in tears.'

A week later she started work in the Ticketing Department. 'The machines were small compared to some of the other machinery and they weren't too noisy. In the Ticketing we had to work several machines at the one time. We each moved to another machine every Monday. If you had a difficult machine you were stuck with it for the rest of the week.'

Bobbins of thread were brought into the department on bogies (wheeled carts) by girls knows as 'bogie girls' and were fed through tubes into the machines, then clamps came down and stuck labels on either end of each bobbin. The workers called it 'top and drop'. If a label was squint, the machinist had to take it off and redo it. 'The gum tasted terrible!'

The machinists were on piecework, and a hundred bobbins could be dealt with in a few minutes. 'If you went home with 30/-. (£1.50p) a week in those days you were rich. I usually earned between 25/- and 32/-.

'The girls used to take faulty bobbins home tied round their waists. They were used as toys and to light fires. In those days there were no tea-breaks.'

Aerial View of Ferguslie Mills 1970s.
Photo Courtesy of Old Paisley Society

Margaret left the mills to get married in 1935, and by the time she returned in 1949 tea-breaks had been introduced, though many pieceworkers still took their tea at their machines because they couldn't afford to stop work.

'We had a dentist in the mills as well as a nurse, and a rest room. And we paid into a holiday fund every week. When the money was due to be paid out our mothers used to give us big safety pins so that we could pin the money into our clothes, to keep it safe until we got home.'

 # Jessie (McMenemy) Lochrie

Jessie McMenemy followed her mother, grandfather, two uncles and three sisters into Ferguslie Mills in 1931, when she was 14 years old. 'It wasn't easy getting a job in the mills, because they paid the best wages in the town.'

There was a crowd of would-be mill-workers waiting at the gatehouse that day and since Jessie was only just over 5 feet in height her mother lifted her up so that she could be seen above the others.

'You're too wee,' said the man who was choosing workers, to which Jessie's mother retorted, 'You're no' very big yourself.' As a result of this bit of cheek, Jessie was taken into the rest room where a nurse checked her hair (to make sure that she did not have lice), as well as her ears, eyes, hands and knickers. Jessie passed the stringent inspection and was put to work in the Twining Department at a starting wage of one pound and tuppence.

The work was hard, and unpleasant. The girls worked in stifling heat and deafening noise, their toes (they had to control the speed of the spools with their big toes) seared by the friction of the machinery. Many of them later suffered foot problems, and Jessie herself eventually lost the big toes on both feet.

Hierarchy

'We shared the mill flat with rats, and worse. When we lifted the big "cheeses" of unbleached cotton down beetles ran out of them and along our arms. The machinery was operated by belts that broke and had to be stapled, then broke again, sometimes lashing back and whipping against the women's arms and shoulders.'

Each mill department had a strict hierarchy, with the women monitored by a supervisor known as the 'mistress'. The mistress answered to the foreman, who answered to the under-manager. Workers had to show extreme deference and a bad supervisor could make his or her department a miserable place to work in. Jessie still feels bitter towards the 'bitch' she suffered under in the learners' flat. 'But there wasn't any animosity or antagonism. It was a matter of survival and hanging onto the job.'

She remembers with fondness, 'the London' - the toilets where six girls would crowd into one cubicle, three perched on the rim and another two with their feet wedged against the walls, so that only one pair of feet could be seen through the space below the door. There, they set each other's hair - using water from the toilet pans since there were no wash hand basins - pierced each other's ears and plucked each other's eyebrows. Jessie was in her 80s when, visiting a club one evening, she heard a voice shrilling, 'Jessie McMenemy, you set my hair out of the toilet pan!'

I Lost Five Shillings From My Pay

Jessie had received a suspension for that incident, (wet hair was a dead give-away). It was her second suspension; the first was for plucking someone's eyebrows during working hours. 'I was suspended for two days, and lost five shillings from my pay. My pal Mary and I sat in the Barshaw Park, afraid to go home and face our mothers.'

Eventually Jessie was moved to the Spooling Department, a 'silk stocking job' where the workers got to keep their shoes on. She was one of the lucky ones, for suspension usually meant a black mark against a worker's record and the danger of less favourable treatment in the future. This was a big worry since many of the mill girls were the chief breadwinners in their families.

At home, pay packets were always handed over intact. 'The only excuse for a broken pay was if there was a collection for someone who had died. When I think of all the folk my sister and I buried! We used to create people and bury them, God forgive me. Really, I was a bit of a rogue!

'It's funny now, looking back on those days, but it wasn't so funny then. It was a hard life. It was slavery. When I left at 20 to get married I swore that no way would a daughter of mine work in the mill.'

During World War 2 conditions improved for the women who worked in the mills, and by the time Jessie returned there to work after the war she found a different regime, one in which the women were more able to speak out, and stand up for themselves.

 # Julia (Fenton) Gilbert

Julia Fenton's first job on leaving school was as a delivery girl in a hat shop, but she hated that, and so, on June 28th 1934 - her mother's birthday - she started work in Ferguslie Mill as a bander, banding threads together and boxing them. She worked in the old Experimental Mill, the nearest building to Newton Street.

'The work was hard and the mills were hot and noisy, but there were shower facilities and during the really hot weather the workers in the spinning mill were given orange juice to drink.' Later, she moved to Examining and then became a warehouse clerkess in Production Control.

Julia recalls the older women teaching embroidery to the girls during work breaks, and she herself eventually went to embroidery classes, paying 2/6d. (12 and a half pence) per term. She also took First Aid classes and worked as a VAD in the mill's first-aid room under the supervision of Sister Davidson, who had been a nurse in World War 1.

During World War 2 Julia was a warden, and she still vividly remembers the night two land mines fell on Paisley, causing many deaths in a first-aid post and also the deaths of two firemen. She and another warden were walking down George Street when they heard a strange rustling noise, like the swish of a crinoline skirt.

Secret Weapon

'There was talk in the town about some secret weapon that searched for bombs, and we thought at first that it might be that. Then the first landmine exploded and we threw ourselves flat on the ground. The cobblestones in the street were actually being lifted up with the blast. When we got to the wardens' post in Storie Street everyone in the place burst out laughing at the sight of us because our faces were completely black with the dust, except for white rings round our eyes and mouths.'

A school friend of Julia's, Maisie Grieve, also worked in the mills. Maisie's grandfather was the grieve at the Coats Mills stables, and at one time, when his family were homeless, they took up temporary residence in the stable tack room.

When Julia first began work in the mill the older workers were still talking about a visit during the First World War from the then Prince of Wales. 'They said his fair hair made his head look like a golden sovereign.'

All Right, Son?

The Coats family all worked in the mills in one capacity or another and Julia recalls them as being 'down-to-earth' and approachable people, willing to sort out any problems their employees might have.

She particularly remembers Peter Coats, who was 'as broad as he was long, with long silver hair. When he went through the mill the senior staff used to compete for the honour of opening the doors for him.

'One day he wanted to look at some machinery, so he brought a three-legged stool with him, to stand on. When he was going through a double door the second door had to be opened as well, to allow for the stool. A mill-worker who happened to be passing by at the time opened the second door for him, saying, "All right, son?" He replied, "Right, lass." The senior staff member went chasing after the mill-worker to give her a row for being so familiar to one of the bosses, and Peter Coats went chasing after him, telling him not to interfere.'

During her time at the mill, Julia joined several of the clubs run by and for mill workers. As a member of the Coats Mill Drama Club, she appeared in a number of plays.

 # An Anonymous Mill Lassie

'I started work in Ferguslie Mills in the 1930s, at the age of 14 and a half, and I worked in the Spooling Department, on the fifth flat. I was a dreamer, I always had been. I used to look out of the window and wish that I was outside, going somewhere.

'I didn't enjoy my time in the mill. It was the claustrophobic atmosphere that I hated. Even if I was sent out on a message to another department I had to get a line from the foreman before I could go.

'You started on timework, then when you got to 16 you went onto piecework. I was put at a table with three women; we were wrapping spools and labelling them. I watched the other women working so hard all the time, trying every minute to get as much done as they could, and I thought, "This isn't for me." I really believe that piecework takes more out of people than they can afford to give.

'I couldn't tell my mother how I felt because she would have wanted me to stay on. So I got a relative who was good at writing letters to do one for me, applying for another job, and I was called for an interview and got the job. Then I told my mother. She wasn't pleased at first, but the work suited me far better. I was away from the mills, away from that claustrophobic feeling, and I was happy.

'Even years later it seems to me that people I still know, who stayed in the mills and stayed on piecework, tend to be a bit jumpy, always hurrying to fit things into their time.'

 # Archie McFarlane

It is only since being asked for reminiscences of my time in the Anchor Mills that I realise how important the Mills and the Clark and Coats family businesses have been in my life and to the well being of my wife and family.

I was born in 1924, the younger of twin boys, at 7 Ross Street, overlooking Anchor recreation grounds. My father was a joiner in the Anchor Mill - later to become foreman joiner. The Anchor Rec Grounds were the pride and joy of Archie Campbell, the head grounds man, who waged constant war on wee boys sneaking in to play or to pinch apples.

When we were seven or eight years old my twin brother Willie and I joined the Anchor Cubs - I think it was the 8th Paisley. I remember David and Jack Ross, the Semple brothers, and Willie and I going through the Rec to the Mile End gatehouse, then through the dining hall grounds to the Cubs headquarters in the old stable building at the rear of the Gassing Mill. The old horse must have hated a Wednesday night!

The Cubs leaders at that time were Bobby Fitch, May Wotherspoon and May Mathie (I was their foreman many years later in the Ticketing Department) and they were always immaculate in full kilts, cream shirts, neckerchiefs, the 'big hat' and lanyards. In the hall we played football and team games, tied knots, made tents and ran about daft!

The Anchor Scouts were Big Time

Following the Cubs we graduated to the Anchor Scouts. They were big time, as they had a football team and a Scout Pipe Band, which was a training ground for the Anchor Mill Pipe Band, a Grade 1 Band. The company supplied all the equipment; pipes, drums, uniforms etc. The officer in charge of the Scouts at that time was Willie Hunter, later to be the manager of the Mile End Mill. Jack Cuthbertson took over at a later date.

Again, the Scout headquarters were in the old stables. We met on a Friday night and it was more like a training ground for terrorists than Scouting. Sliding down a flight of stairs on a tea tray, wee boys hanging by their belts from coat hooks on the wall, games where you risked life and limb for points for your patrol. I remember that the wet sawdust used when sweeping the floor was thrown everywhere *but* on the floor. The dust was like a fog in the hall when we swept up at the end of our evenings!

Anchor Mills Joiners' Shop staff. Foreman William McFarlane, right of back row, retired in 1957.
Photo Courtesy of Archie McFarlane

Sma' Shot Parades and Jamborees

On Sma' Shot Day we formed up at the main gate and marched behind the Scout Pipe Band to Gilmour Street Station to join a train for Troon or Ayr. We had jamborees in the Half Timers' School at Ferguslie and Hallowe'en parties in the dining hall. Girl Guides were our guests - I think! We were paying more attention to the pies and dumpling prepared by Maggie Taylor, one of the cooks. Jimmie McMillan was the janitor.

Round camp fires at the end of our evening we sang songs that are still remembered and loved, and have been sung at many a real camp fire in many parts of the world. Friendships made at that time have lasted and stood the test of time - today it would be called 'bonding'.

On leaving school I got a job with Graham, the lithographers. They printed tickets and labels for the mills, and were one of the many small companies dependent on the mills for work.

I started working in the Anchor Mills Packing Department late 1939 or early 1940, when I was about 16 years old. The department was in the bottom flat of the Finishing Mill and three of us started together - Bert Muir, Alex Muir and myself. A young lady, Maisie McLean, fixed us up with a cup of tea on that first day, and I'm pleased to say we're still friends to this day. (Alex Muir went on to the Glasgow office, and during the war Bert Muir and I met up again when he was a crew member on a Sunderland flying boat that landed in bad weather on Lough Neagh in the North of Ireland in 1943.)

As the 'boy' in Packing Department one of my jobs was to draw all the blackout curtains - every windowpane was covered in a lace-like material and varnished to protect the glass from bomb blast. All the younger men were going off to the Forces and being replaced with older men, and in many instances the girls were doing what had been a man's job, such as tenting etc.

Mill Fire Watchers

There was a war on and all male employees were expected to take their turn at fire watching. Air raid shelters were built in the dining hall grounds and sirens were installed on the Finishing Mill roof. The dining hall was the headquarters; you came in to the mill about 7 p.m. till 6 a.m., and you and a partner were allocated a firewatch area - the roof of the Gassing, Box Shop, Finishing Mill etc., as I remember - and you stayed at that post all night.

Later, beds were provided in the counting house and dining hall training room and you only had to turn out if the sirens sounded. The standard payment for a fire watch shift was 7/6d. (37 ½ pence).

There would be about 20 men on each shift and the shifts covered 7 nights per week. If you were passing the mill when the siren sounded you could go in as a volunteer. If the All Clear sounded an hour later you got to go home and you were still paid your 7/6d!

At this time we worked 7.30 a.m. to 5.30 p.m. Monday to Friday, Saturdays 7.30 a.m. to 12 noon. Most weeks there was Tuesday and Thursday overtime till 7.30 p.m. For this you were rewarded with a free iced bun (tea breaks were 10 minutes morning and afternoon).

No Whistling And No Bare Legs!

It was blackout, the weather was cold and wet, some air raids lasted all night, and there was rationing on top of everything else - it was a credit to all workers that though sometimes late they were seldom absent. I think my wages at this time were about £2.10/-. (£2.50p) per week.

The Finishing Mill manager was Arthur Phipps - a bowler hat and a rolled umbrella. We were not allowed to whistle in his presence and he would only employ girls who wore stockings.

Up to this point I had been attending night school in the Camphill School. The company paid all your fees and books etc. Many of the night school evenings were spent in the Kelburne or the Astoria Cinemas. It didn't do much for your woodwork skills but it was warm and more enjoyable!

In 1942 I turned 18, and joined RAF Coastal Command. My brother Willie and I only met once during the war, when he was on a short leave from the Army. In 1947 I was demobilised and returned to the Anchor Mills Packing Department. All the blokes that I remember came back except Bert Muir's brother Tom, a ticketing tenter.

After the war the mills were going full blast; we were sending thread for finishing to mills abroad, and finished goods to home and export markets. Horse-drawn carts were being loaded with packing cases and cartons for the docks and far off markets all round the world.

Meantime, I applied for and got a job as a ticketing tenter. We were all young men just back from the Forces. Bob McDonald was the senior man, and also Pipe Major - or he may have been the Sergeant Piper - in the Mill Pipe Band. James Guy was sub-manager and A. Turner was foreman at Papering and Boxing. Charlie Sellers was foreman at the machine end.

We had a mixed social club and paid in 1/- (5p) per week. We went to shows and had days out and parties in a room in the dining hall; all good clean fun without a drink in sight. At one time we were employing displaced persons (DPs) refugees from Europe in the Ticketing Department. They were living in a big house or hostel in Bridge of Weir and came in on special buses. There were no Miss Worlds among them! They were very hard workers, producing quantity rather than quality. The girls in the department were very good to them in many a quiet way.

The Recreation Club

At this period, around 1949, the machines were all driven by overhead belts with the lighting high in the roof so it was a transformation when new lighting was installed, and overhead shafts and belts replaced by individual motors. The volume of work was such that dispersal units were set up in Banton and London Road, where local labour was available.

Anchor Ladies Hockey 1st Eleven, 1922/1923.   Photo Courtesy of the Old Paisley Society.

Anchor Ladies Hockey Team, 1929/1930.   Photo Courtesy of the Old Paisley Society.

The Recreation Club came into its own when we got back from the Forces. Cricket, hockey, tennis, badminton, bowling, everything but football - all were now available on our own doorstep for a mere 10/- (50p) a year. There was even a golf section, of which I am a founder member. The Recreation Club and its amenities were the best in the West of Scotland. There were plunge baths, showers, tearooms and changing rooms, all spotless - but no bar! The company supplied all the sports equipment free and if you wanted to play any sport you just had to turn up.

Albert Smallwood was employed as a professional cricket coach in the early days of the club and later employed within the company. Dances were a regular feature in the main hall - 2/6d. (12 and a half pence) - and still no bar. The sports section dances were an annual event, when long frocks and dinner suits were the thing. Tickets cost about 10/- (50p). 'The Anchor' always meant a good night at the dancing.

The recreation club was a meeting place for all employees in the company, whether they worked in Glasgow or Paisley, and lasting relationships and good companions were met and made at the Rec.

About 1950, D. Ross and I were promoted from ticketing tenter to spooling tenter, which meant a mega-rise of 10/- a week. D. Ross went to Conant Spooling and I went to the Weilds Spooling. This machine produced 10 spools at a time.

A Shock to the System

It was a shock to the system in more ways than one. In the 5th flat the noise was shocking and the tenters in general were older men and a bit mean on the information regarding tenting. The only male toilets were on the bottom floor - five flats down and back up again!

I was just getting to grips with the Spooling Machine tenting when Larry McBride and I were moved to the new mechanised Spooling Experimental Unit in the old Embroidery Mill. Eight spooling machines had been overhauled and converted to automatic loading and doffing. In essence, only three girls were needed to look after five mechanised machines i.e., 50 spindles - while with the old method it would have taken about 10 girls to look after 50 spindles, (this is just a generalisation depending on many factors of length, speeds, specifications, etc.)

In the meantime, the Finishing Mill had a facelift. New floors, lights, toilets and cloakrooms for staff and workers were put in, as well as new elevators. The mill was painted from top to bottom. The floors were like dance halls and the cloakrooms like those in a hotel, with a mixed canteen on the bottom flat.

Double shift operation and mechanised spooling were the way forward. We were moved from the Experimental Unit to the third flat Finishing and it was decided that all other spooling machines were to be mechanised as soon as possible.

At this time (1951/1952) I was promoted to foreman and joined Archie Kelly (of Motherwell and Hearts football clubs) in what was to be the third flat Spooling Department. This was a mammoth change aimed at taking the old spooling practices out of the Ark and into a new bright exciting era.

An Efficient and Well-organised Department

Mr Gilbert Greensmith (he was English but we never held that against him!) was an assistant manager and involved in all aspects of the new Spooling Department. He was an expert in system and methods, maths and statistics. During this period Gilbert must have - and not for lack of forward planning - had fresh problems to solve every day. Regardless, he was always a gentleman and never failed to thank you or other sections that did a job for him.

When the transformation was complete - and it had taken some time - everyone involved could take great pride in a very efficient and well-organised department.

Some years later Mr Greensmith's retiral presentation was held in the Recreation Club. It was the best-attended presentation ever in the history of the Finishing Mill. It was indeed a night to remember.

In the mill, female supervisors were known as Mistresses. Once the Fault Removing Mistress who worked for me was in hospital and I visited her. The minister was visiting her as well, and she told him, 'I've been Mr McFarlane's Mistress for years.'

The desk girls were wonderful. A good desk girl was the foreman's right hand woman, worth her weight in gold.

Chapping

It was a tradition that Hallowe'en night on the late shift always produced a 'guyser' dressed up for the occasion - as a fairy, footballer, ballet-dancer or the manager. I remember an all-action Charleston dancer, long beads and garters as well, who toured the flats with a can, collecting for Erskine Hospital.

Another Mill custom was 'chapping' when a girl was leaving to be married, etc. As she went forward for her final pay the others would beat on the table or any available surface to make a noise. So between chapping and cheering, she got a rousing send off.

There was a strict no-smoking rule; no swearing was an unwritten law and well observed by everyone. That was 20-odd years ago.

As a foreman my first annual salary was £404, or £37 a month. In 1953 I married into money - my wife worked for R. Cochran & Son, (now Arnotts) full time and all day Saturday for £4 per week, and had to dress in black - no wonder! At this time we bought our first house, back in Ross Street where I was born.

In the early 1960s I was seconded to the Fleming Reid Scots Wool Shop/Knitting Factory in Greenock. I was given two weeks' organisation and method training before going to assist the factory manager to get the garments off the factory floor and into the shops.

With a lot of hard work from everyone we managed to overcome the problems, then three years down the line the parent company sold all the shops and converted the knitting factory into a yarn production unit.

Foreman Joiner William McFarlane (2nd right), father of Archie and Willie McFarlane, instructing young mill employees during an evening class in the Anchor Joiner's Shop.
Photo Courtesy of Archie McFarlane

I returned to Anchor to look after trainees, tenter training and experimental work in the Training Room for the Finishing Mill manager, Mr. A. Rowan; just in time to get involved in the changeover from wooden to plastic spools.

About 1966/67, J. Kerr and Robert McGhee and I were sent down to the British Industrial Plastics factory in Birmingham to be introduced to the plastic injection moulding machines and the essential moulds. The package and changeover must have cost millions. Three machines were delivered and installed in the Coffin End in Ferguslie Mills and were later transferred to the Plastic Moulding Department back in the bottom flat of Anchor Finishing - the old Packing Department from where I had started my career in the mill. This was a brand new operation to Anchor Mills, like starting up a plastic moulding business from scratch - training of all operators, production records, systems and methods, stock controls; and each new multi-cavity spool mould received - they could weigh about half a tonne each - had to be commissioned.

Every Move a Challenge

Conditions could be hot, with the smell of hot plastic in the atmosphere. The Foreman Electrician was William Patrick and the Foreman Engineer was Gilbert Shields, both first-class tradesmen.

A total of 22 injection moulding machines were finally installed and worked on a 3-shift basis, starting on a Sunday night at 10 p.m. till the following Friday. All types of thread supports were produced for home mills and exported to other mills abroad. It was an all-male operation.

In 1981 I was given the opportunity to take early retirement along with 24 other 'senior soldiers', and retired in October of that year.

You would think that 42 years with the same company would be a bit of a bore - not so, as you were moved around a variety of charges, each one a new challenge within and outside the Finishing Mill. So life was never dull or boring. My claims to fame? I learned to read Bill Chittick's writing, and I once assembled an MFI wardrobe in four days!

I would like to dedicate these memories of mine to all the mill girls who worked so hard in the Finishing Mill. I am very proud to be associated with all of them.

Archie McFarlane, Finishing Foreman, Ticketing, Spooling and Plastic Moulding Departments of Anchor Mills.

 # Willie McFarlane

Willie McFarlane and his twin brother Archie were born in Ross Street, overlooking the Anchor recreation grounds, in 1924. Their father was a joiner in the Mill, later to become foreman joiner.

'We went to the South Public School. The "public" bit is important,' stresses Willie, who has a lively sense of humour. 'Once when I was abroad, another Paisley worker - a woman who had also been a pupil at the South School - and I were in the company of some English people. When the woman said that she went to a public school in Paisley they were impressed because in England, a public school is what we would call a private school.

'I said, "Do you know, I went to the very same public school!" She could have killed me!'

Anchor Mills Balling and Packing staff in the 1950s, with Willie McFarlane, far right, back row.
Photo Courtesy of Willie McFarlane

27

When he first started work in Anchor Mills Willie was sent to the Hank Winding Department, where he became a tenter. Like his brother, he enjoyed his work. 'As a tenter, I might be passing a machine and the woman working it would ask for my help and I would give it. Then I was told that this wasn't the right way of it - the women were supposed to come to the bench and ask for a tenter if she needed help. There was one woman known to the tenters as the Hawkhead bus because she arrived at the bench every ten minutes.

"Peein' Cronies"

Willie McFarlane (3rd left, front row) with fellow members of
Anchor Mills Men's Hockey Team.
Photo Courtesy of Willie McFarlane

'The mill lassies were great ones for going to the toilets with their pals. We called them the "peein' cronies" because they used to wave to each other from their workplace, and then proceed to the toilets arm in arm, "cleeking" each other.

'As younger employees we got up to all sorts of mischief. There was a very strict man who worked the hoist - he always had it in for the lads, and we had our methods of retaliation. He used to settle into a cubicle in the toilets every morning at a certain time. The cistern was on the half-landing above, and there was a six-inch gap between the toilet doors and the floor. Once he was settled, one of the lads would flush the toilet from upstairs while another threw a bucket of water under the door. We wondered why he used to hit us!

'I remember Mr Phipps, the manager of the Balling Department, sending for me and Robert Molloy and telling us, "Stick in at the work and leave the girls alone." I would have preferred it the other way around!'

During World War Two Willie's twin Archie went into the RAF and so did their other brother, while Willie himself went into the Army. 'When a woman in a tramcar asked my mother during the war if she had any sons in the Services, she said, "Yes, three - two in the RAF and one serving."'

The Cruelty Men

After the war Willie returned to the mill where he became a balling tenter, and in 1951 he became a foreman. 'I was in charge of 60 women and we got on all right.'

After spending several years as foreman, Willie became a "cruelty man." 'The proper term was Work Study Engineer - a rate fixer. Nobody liked the rates fixers. I was told that I had been given the job because I got on well with folk and they thought that I might give the position a better image among the workers. Then after a year I was taken off it because they thought that I was too friendly with the workers!'

Then Willie was sent abroad. His first trip overseas posting was to Portugal, then to a small mill in Hong Kong, followed by a year in Indonesia, setting up a new factory. 'They went in for bribery in a big way in Indonesia. Once when the boiler broke down and we got it up and running again the local inspector refused to pass it as working properly. Without it, we were ruined, so he was offered a job as our boiler inspector at an annual salary of £10. He accepted the job, and passed the boiler there and then.'

Willie was also instrumental in setting up a new factory in Malaysia. 'The machinery for these factories had to be taken from the floors of the Anchor Mills and shipped out.' Then came a move to Thailand, followed by a spell in Colombia, where he shared a flat with Brian Coats, the last member of the Coats family to work within the company. Colombia was a dangerous place for foreigners, and when he wanted to move about outside the mills Willie had to be extremely careful.

When he was sent to Turkey his wife Ethel, who had worked in the canteen at Anchor Mills, went with him. 'We were the only two Europeans in a town the size of Paisley. Life was hard, as Turkey was in an economic slump so there were no luxuries. There was a shortage of everything and when we went to Cyprus for a break we took back 12 tins of baked beans and four packets of Bisto - luxury!

'People think that it must be romantic, travelling all over the world, but for me, the best time of my working life was spent in Paisley.

Willie McFarlane and his wife Ethel, who worked in the canteen at Anchor Mills, pictured on their wedding day. Willie's twin brother Archie was his best man.
Photo Courtesy of Willie McFarlane

They All Knew a Coats Man

'Working abroad can be lonely, especially when you don't know the language. Not that it was always a drawback. I mind going into a bar in one of the places I had been sent to, and two fitters from Plats, a company that made machinery and worked with Coats and had been in South America for three years, invited me to have a drink with them. I asked if they knew the local language, and one of them said, "no bother," then he held up three fingers and shouted "Beer." It worked.'

There were various ways of easing homesickness. 'When I was working in Indonesia boxes of material used to come in from Paisley and one day an Indonesian worker brought me a folder that had arrived in one of the boxes. It contained a copy of the Dandy, sent out to me by my brother Archie.

'If you worked for Coats, you were known wherever you went in the world as a Coats man. The Paisley influence and the Paisley way of speaking was spread all over the world by the Coats workers. Once when I was in Turkey and one of the machines broke down we had to call in a Brazilian tenter, a Mr Piano, who had been trained in Paisley. He was a lovely man.

When we met up in the mill I asked, "How's No. 2 machine?" and he said, "Oh, it's away ta-ta, Willie." It was strange! Here I was in a Turkish mill with a Brazilian saying in a broad Paisley accent, "It's away ta-ta, Willie." It was a humorous and special moment.

"That's a lum hat!"

Once, at a training session for foreign workers in Paisley, Jimmy Ross, a Conant tenter, was showing the trainees what a 1000-yard glacé spool should look like. He held it up, with its shiny black thread, and said, "Look at that - a lum hat!" We just knew that all over the world, wherever there were Coats mills, these people would be saying to their workers, "That's a lum hat!"

After Turkey, Willie was sent back to Portugal, then to Austria and finally to South Africa. 'I retired from South Africa, but then I was called back and went to Jamaica, Trinidad and Venezuela before retiring for good.

'In my time as a Coats man abroad I was present during three revolutions, one in Trinidad and two in Bangkok. I once asked a local resident during a revolution how they knew which were the good guys and which were the bad guys and was told, "The ones with the guns are the good guys."'

Willie wasn't the first McFarlane to become a Coats man abroad. 'My uncle, Andrew McFarlane, a Conant tenter, worked at the Coats mills in Russia just before the revolution, and later he was sent to Montreal, where he settled.'

Very Special People

Like his brother Archie, Willie McFarlane has nothing but praise for the women who worked the machines in the thread mills, and it still rankles with him that when the staff were granted an extra week's holiday, the same privilege was not extended to the workers in the flats.

'It meant that the newest and youngest staff member was immediately entitled to an extra week off every year, and yet women who had been there for years were denied the same right. This was rectified around 1960.

'There were good times, and not so good times, but where I would never tell them to their faces, to my mind the girls in the mills, both in Paisley and in all these other countries, were very special people - so special that I married one!'

Nan (Stewart) Doe

When she left Abercorn School at the age of 14 Nan Stewart began work in the Twisting Department of Ferguslie Mills. It was the mid-thirties, and 'in those days you had to take what you got. My mother needed my pay.' Her three sisters were all mill workers, two in the Cotton Mill and one in the Counting House.

After going to the rest room for the medical examination that all mill workers had to go through before being accepted, Nan learned the rules then got down to work. 'It was noisy, but you just had to get adjusted to it.'

Nan worked her way up to the position of 6-sider, a twiner who could run three double-sided machines at once. She stayed in the department for 39 years, mainly working the early shift, from 6 a.m. to 2 p.m.

'It suited another worker, a friend of mine, to work the 2-10 p.m. shift, so we fitted in together. I lived in Gallowhill, and I quite enjoyed the early-morning walk to the mills at Ferguslie. Getting up early was never a problem for me.'

The early shift, which meant finishing work at 2 p.m., also gave Nan the time she needed to follow her main hobby. A keen supporter of Paisley's very successful ice-hockey team, the Paisley Pirates, she was able to attend all their games, following them to away events.

'I have no complaints about my time in Ferguslie Mill. The work was hard, but I made good friends you couldn't have met nicer people anywhere - and we still keep in touch.'

When Nan first started work in the mills the supervisors were all males, but eventually women began to be promoted to the post.

'Some foremen and forewomen were easier to work with than others, but all in all, if you did your work well they didn't bother you. I remember Robert Thomson was one of the foremen, and I had Jenny Leitch and Sadie Fairlie as forewomen later on. They were all good people to work with.'

 # Alice Elliott

Alice was the Dux at St Catherine's School, but her mother could not afford to keep her on at the school, so when she reached 14 she started work at Ferguslie Mills in 1937. They put her into the Papering Department because she was too wee to reach the spools.

Like most of the mill lassies, Alice handed her entire wage packet to her mother, receiving pocket money in return. When she married (she continued to work after marriage because it was wartime) her first wage packet as a married woman went to her mother because she had been living at home when she earned it. 'In those days you stayed with your mother until you married, and she ruled the roost. My mum was good, but you didn't get much pocket money.'

Alice got a shilling, which she spent on such items as silk stocking and sweets. She was also expected to put something by to pay for the week's holiday the family enjoyed every year at Largs or West Kilbride. By 1950 her pocket money had risen to the less-than-heady sum of 12/6d. (63½ pence)

Alice loved being a mill girl and has happy memories. 'You were always in a crowd, you were very seldom alone. I made lifelong friends there, and I remember being taught to crochet by the spinsters, and curling my hair with a clothes pin and a Kirby grip, and going to the pictures with my pals after work.' Being only 4 feet 10 inches, Alice got in for everything half-price.

'Never trust a fella, Ella.'

She remembers the theatre runs organised by the mills, the mill trips to Blackpool illuminations, teasing the foreman who dyed his hair. Buying on tick from Annie Hutton, who smuggled tuppenny cakes of chocolate into

Employees of Anchor and Ferguslie Mills at Douglas Bridge Harvest Camp, Cockburnspath, near Dunbar. September 1950.
Photo Courtesy of Old Paisley Society

the mill in her drawers. Telling her friend Ella, when she was disappointed in love, 'Never trust a fella, Ella.' It was to be scrawled in dozens of Christmas cards throughout the following years.

Then there were the rituals such as 'Skittery Winter', where the last girl into work on Hogmanay was greeted with a deafening din of spools clattered against the shelves. And the fuss they made the day you left to get married, decorating your coat with crepe paper and running you up and down the street, making a racket with pan lids.

When it was her turn, Ella took 20 of her best friends for a meal at the Ice Rink, then on to the Paisley Theatre where the singer sang her favourite song, *When You Were Sweet Sixteen*. And later, her pals made her jump over a chanty filled with dolls.

And then there was 'cleeking' your pals to and from work, and having a chinwag and a fly puff in 'the

London' the name given to the mill toilets.

'I remember that the washerwoman who used to scrub the floors sat in the Londons, and there was an old Irish woman who used to tell us all the tales.

'You really lived then, you really laughed. There were singsongs too. There was always a crowd of pals. I feel sorry for the kids nowadays - I do.'

 # Elsie (Watson) Pollock

'I had to stay on at school until I was 14 and a half because my birthday, on February 21ˢᵗ, came one week after the time allowed. When I did leave I had hoped to get a job at Dobie's Tobacco Factory, where the pay was good, but there was no joy for me. '

Instead, Elsie got a job in the weaving mill at Underwood Road, near her home.

'The pay was very low, and worse still, I had to sit beside four women near retirement age, and learn how to darn any flaws found in the cloth. I hated it because I wanted to be with young people of my own age. I had two sisters who worked in the Anchor Finishing Mill, and they told me to go to the gate opposite the East End Park on Monday morning because Clarks were taking on staff.

'On the Monday I joined about 18 girls, all looking for jobs. First they called out the names of five girls who had been spoken for, then they said, "Put up your hand if you want to go to the twining at the Mile End Mill." Needless to say, my hand was up right away and in I went. I was earning the equivalent of £1.04p a week, and I was rich!'

Cool in Summer, Cold in Winter

The money was very welcome, for Elsie's father and oldest brother couldn't find work, and like most of the mill girls she gave every penny she earned to her mother.

'In the Twining Department we worked in our bare feet because the thread was run through water. Big sheets ran the length of the machines to catch the water and prevent us from slipping. Because of the water it was cool in the summer, but cold work in the winter.

'I was only in the mill for three days when I was called before Mr McAlpine, the sub-manager. The weaving mill had complained about me leaving without permission. I said that I couldn't tell them because I hadn't had time to let them know I had a new job.

Mr McAlpine asked how much I had earned at the weaving mill and when I told him they had paid me four shillings (20p) a week he nearly exploded. "Good God, lassie," he said, "get back to your work and leave this to me." And I never heard any more about it.'

A Frightening Moment

It was Mr McAlpine who later asked the young twiner if she would like to learn to play hockey. Elsie decided that she would, and became a member of the Anchor Mills hockey team. 'I loved it!'

Elsie did well at the job, until one day when she had gone in early to get her machine ready for doffing. 'It was our job to fill the empty spindles but sometimes when they came to us they still had some thread on them. We weren't allowed to use knifes or razor blades to cut the thread off in case it splintered the spindles, but it took a long time to pull thread from a basket of spindles. On that day I was cutting the thread away with a razor blade when I saw a shadow. It was the foreman, Mr Mack, and when I looked up he held his hand out for the blade, then walked away without a word.

'I expected to be in big trouble but I never heard any more about it. I'm sure he realised why I was cutting the thread. He was a lovely man and everyone liked him.'

'Later on I was moved to the Pacific Mill, where Bob Wilson was the foreman. We had good days and bad days there. I was working four machines and the thread was like spider webs. When it rained and the wind blew it was very difficult to work with and as a result it was just work, work, work all the time. When I asked Bob for help he put me onto a change of job.

'This time I was working with thread as thick as string. It ran through water, which made it even stronger. I had to break it over my knee, and that made my fingers all red and sore.

'I remember being terrified of our forewoman; she was quite a frightening person. One of the women could read the cards and when we were in the toilets the girls used to get her tell their fortunes. She told me that someone didn't like me, and I was convinced that she meant the forewoman!'

From the Mills to Ghana

Elsie left the mill when she married at 21 years of age, but returned to work not long after.

'We moved in with my husband's parents, and I really missed the mill and my friends there. So I went back - I suppose you could say that it was a choice between my friends and my mother-in-law!

'They were good friends. About six of us worked the 6-2 and 2-10 shifts and we used to meet up and sit on the grass to have our lunch. I mind that Jenny Buchanan and Isa Gilligan were two of them. And there was Cathy Harper, who lived near me; we walked to work together every day, and now the two of us go together to the Salvation Army Pensioners' Club. Oh, we had happy times in the mills.'

Eventually Elsie's husband went to work in Ghana, and the family settled there. With no school nearby she taught her own children, and eventually became headmistress of a small school with 20 children.

'I enjoyed teaching them. I liked school myself, and my parents were keen on education. I remember my father taking us for walks, and teaching us to recite the alphabet backwards. I can still do it.'

 # Jenny Leitch

Jenny Leitch was fond of sewing, and when she turned 14, her parents wanted her to try for a job in the Co-operative Tailoring Department. But Jenny insisted on working in Ferguslie Mills, where her father was an oiler in the Mechanical Department. He also had the task of ringing the big mill bell that summoned the workers every morning at 7 a.m. and again at 7.15 a.m., then at 12 noon for the dinner break.

Every morning Jenny went along to the mill gates at 7.15 a.m. to wait with other girls who were looking for work. When her turn came she was taken to the first aid room, where all new starts were checked to make sure that they did not have lice, then given a position in the Twisting Department. There, she had to learn the department's rules off by heart before being given a calico apron and handed over to a machinist for training.

'The twisting machines were noisy and we had to work in our bare feet. After World War 2 we were given ear plugs and plastic shoes, and overalls in place of the calico aprons.' The pay was good - Jenny started on £1.0.6d. a week, while a friend working in a Paisley joiner's office got 7/6d. (about 37p).

The Ferguslie Bell, which once rang to summon the mill workers, is now a feature in the courtyard garden at the Sma' Shot Cottages.
Photo Courtesy of Old Paisley Society

When the girls in the department felt that they deserved a pay rise, it was Jenny who wrote the letter to the manager. 'Everyone signed it, but of course the manager only had to compare the signatures with handwriting of the actual letter. He sent for me and asked if I had written it. I said I had, and he said that he would give us an extra 6d. a week. When I told my parents what I had done, they were horrified!'

After WW2 Jenny became a Welfare Officer in the mill, then she moved to the Training Section for her final six years before retirement.

 # Alex Greer

Alex Greer's plan to go to University after completing his education at Paisley Grammar School ended when his father died suddenly in 1941. Instead, Alex went to Coats' Central Agency in Glasgow, the first person to go into the Agency without School Higher qualifications. He worked in the Production Standards Department, which set wage rates.

'I started as an office boy and when I left to go into the Navy three years later I was still an office boy. There was no quick promotion in those days.'

Returning to Scotland after the war he moved to the Insurance and Shipping Department, then after a training course he ended up in Sales, spending time in the Manchester, Leicester and Leeds offices before returning to Head Office in the 1950s.

'I worked in the Thread Advisory Service, advising customers on the correct threads required for the new materials that had come in after the war. Nylon thread, for instance, caused problems where stretching was concerned. Our research laboratory helped to solve this by breaking up and re-spinning the thread, but by that time sewing machines had become much faster, generating enough heat in some instances to melt the nylon thread. Coats came up with a core thread, providing an outer layer of cotton which absorbed the heat and protected the synthetic inner layer.'

IRA Bombing

Alex's job entailed visiting customers' factories, writing advertising material 'blurb' for newspapers, and attending exhibitions. 'At that time Coats made their own zip fasteners, in Brazil and South America, while in Britain ICI made and sold Lightning Fasteners. Coats struck a deal with them whereby we sold their Lightning Fasteners to the home market and sold our own fasteners abroad. I was moved to the Scottish Depot in Ferguslie, the base for the Scottish sales of fasteners, where we dealt with the domestic side - thread, fasteners, etc. After that the depot moved to Kinning Park in Glasgow, the central warehouse that dispensed Coats products to depots all over the world.

'At that time the various depot managers dealt with materials entering and leaving their depots, but when Coats bought over the London firm of Pickaby, a big haberdashery concern that sold pins and needles, bindings, tapes, velcros, etc., it was decided that we needed a Credit Controller, and I was offered the job.'

His training session in London was brief, but memorable. 'That was when the IRA first bombed London. I was near enough to hear the explosion and the emergency services' sirens, but it wasn't until I got back to my hotel room that I found out what had happened.'

After a few years as Credit Controller, a job he enjoyed, Alex's career with Coats came to a premature end when he became ill, and had to take early retirement in 1978. 'By then the Ferguslie Mills side of the business was beginning to close down and there were a lot of changes.'

The Philatelic Club

Among the many clubs and organisations within the mills was the Philatelic Club, founded in the 1950s after a relative of the then Secretary pointed out that with some 600 letters passing through the Head Office mailroom every day from all over the world, the stamps would be well worth collecting. Alex was appointed as curator of the club in 1957 with a Mounting Committee of six people, each looking after one geographical area of the world.

'The committee members changed over the years, but I remained curator and in 1992 I had the task of presenting the collection we had amassed to Paisley Museum on permanent loan.'

 # Nessie (Craig) Burns

Nessie Craig's parents both worked in Nether Common Carpet Works in Paisley, her father as a weaver and her mother as a printer, but by the time she left Abercorn School at 14 years of age, Nessie had decided that she wanted to work in the Anchor Thread Mills.

'My cousin worked there, and she spoke up for me. It was 1941, and I was sent to the Spooling, on the 5th flat of Anchor Mill (now known as the Domestic Finishing Mill, the building still stands by the Hammills and is a town landmark). I worked as a spooler's helper, which meant that as the bobbins were filled I had to clear them off the machine and put them into a big wooden tray, which was then placed at the end of the machine, ready to be taken to the warehouse. I also had to cut the ends of thread from the bobbins. We had small scissors for that job, and we had a special way of using them. We used to slip one pinky through one of the handles, and use our thumbs and forefingers to open and shut the blades. This was much faster than the usual way.

Working at Top Speed

'I had to work at top speed all the time, because if I fell behind I kept the spooler back, and she wasn't happy about that. The idea was that the spoolers shared the job of cutting the threads with their helpers, but often the helpers had to do the lot. While you were carrying the boards of bobbins to the end of the machine the next lot were piling up, waiting to be trimmed and taken away. I hated that job, trying to keep up was a continual anxiety. And then on Fridays we stopped early to clean the machines, and as the helper, I had to get down on the floor and clean the really dirty part of the machinery.'

Her father was able to make her work a little easier. He made a little penknife that snipped off the threads faster than scissors and was also great for cleaning oil and threads from the machinery.

There were no unions in the Paisley mills at that time, but one day when Nessie and her pals were leaving the mill they met some union representatives at the gate. "They told us that while the spoolers earned good money, we weren't earning as much as we deserved. They pointed out that without us, the spoolers wouldn't be able to work and said that if we came out on strike they would negotiate with the management and get better wages for us. They made it all sound so wonderful, so we agreed.'

Nessie's mother didn't quite see it that way. 'When I went home to Gallowhill and told her that I was on strike she said, "No you're not, you can just put your coat on and get back to work." And I said, "But they won't let me - they said we had to stay out until they got more money for us!"

Not Very Popular

'After a day or two the union said that they had won and we could go back. We got a pay rise, but we weren't very popular with the spoolers, who had lost money while we were out. I think they would have liked to send us all to Coventry, but they didn't dare in case we went out on strike again!'

The highlight of Nessie's young life arrived when she became 18 and was given her own machine. 'I was so happy - now I was working for myself and I could stop the machine if I needed to, instead of having to rush to keep up all the time.'

Again, Nessie's father was of great help. 'When the rods holding the spools had to be slackened off, the tenters did the job with special keys. If the tenter was busy with another machine you had to wait for him, which slowed you down. My father asked me to let him see one of the keys, but I couldn't take one home, so I got hold of one, dipped it in oil and then pressed it onto a sheet of paper. I also drew the key, and from the drawing and the oily outline, he made me a key so that I could loosen the nuts myself.'

The thread was waxed as it was spooled, and in those days, the wax came in the form of two sticks similar to candles. The thread ran between them and the tension had to be just right; if it was too tight, it could slice right through the wax. 'The only break we got was when the waxes needed renewing - we had to go to the tower, on the next floor, to get more waxes. But even then you were timed, so you couldn't loiter for too long. We were on piecework, which meant that if your machine was switched off you lost money.'

In later machines the waxes were replaced by trays of a liquid, milky substance.

Time for a Change

After five years as a mill worker Nessie decided that it was time for a change. 'The work was monotonous and I was beginning to get fed up with it. At that time everyone was still on war work and the alternative was to go into munitions, but I didn't want to do that. Then a friend who worked for Scottish Cables suggested that I should try them. I applied, and because of the training I had been given at the mill, I landed a job as an inspectress.

'My real ambition was to be a nurse, but because I had had a major operation when I was younger my mother felt that nursing would be too heavy a job for me. But I took First Aid classes while I was in the mill.

'Now, I can look back at my time in the mills and remember the good times and the laughs, and forget the days when I wished that I didn't have to go to work. We used to save up for nights out - a meal at Danny Brown's in Glasgow, followed by a visit to the King's Theatre, or the Empire. A great night out.'

One of Nessie's less happy memories is of a foreman, 'a big man, who always insisted on calling me "Ag-nes." I didn't like it at all and I told him again and again that although I was christened Agnes, my name was Nessie, and I had never been called Agnes in my life, but he persisted. I can still remember him shouting, "Ag-nes!" I hated that!

'I learned a lot at the mills, possibly more than I should have. I remember there was a book going around while I was there, it was called "The Red Lights" and everyone was reading it. I got a copy and I was sitting reading it in the house when my brother called me out of the room and told me that I shouldn't be reading it in front of my mother.

'I said, "But everyone's reading it." I couldn't think why my brother was so horrified. I asked my dad what he thought and he asked if I understood the book. I said "No, but when I come to a bit I don't understand I just turn the page." I was young and naive - the book was about venereal disease!'

Nessie went back to the mills after she was married, but only stuck it for five weeks. 'They were all mechanised by then and I couldn't bear it.'

She then became a nursing auxiliary, finally achieving her lifelong ambition, but had to give it up because she slipped two discs in her back. As her mother had foretold years earlier, the work had been too heavy for her. She then became a nursery assistant, a job she greatly enjoyed.

Isobel Berrie

Isobel Berrie started work in the Anchor Mill straight from school, when she was 14 years of age. 'It was in 1941. My mother had worked in the Spooling Department and she spoke to the foreman and got me in.'

Isobel was started in the Ticketing warehouse. 'It was like a shop, and I worked at a table. I was there for 11 years, and I loved the job. I got married in 1950 and left in 1952 to start my family.'

She returned to the mill several years later, and this time she was sent to the old Embroidery Mill, where she worked with colour cards. 'We assembled the cards that went into shops to show all the colours of the embroidery threads. I was there for 10 years, and again, I enjoyed the work. I thought that the wages were good, and I have never regretted the day I started work in the mill.

'The social life was terrific. We went to the Anchor Rec a lot. They had showers and baths that we could use, and of course there were the dances. We were all members. There was table tennis as well, and most of my friends were mill workers too. We used to go skating together, and on the trips to different places. I still see Pat Skinneder, she worked in Ticketing at the same time as me.

King George VI and Queen Elizabeth during a tour of
Ferguslie Mills in 1942.
Photo Courtesy of Old Paisley Society

'I remember when the present Queen's parents came to Paisley, and seeing the late Queen Mother walking through the Ticketing Department.

'I still have an affection for the mill,' said Isobel, who was made redundant in 1983. 'I remember 6d. being taken off my wages for Erskine Hospital, and money taken off for holidays and the pension, which I benefit from today.

'During the war we also had money taken off our wages for the munitions. We were given extra coupons because we made thread for the Army, Navy and Air Force, so we were classed as a reserved occupation.'

 # Alex McKinnon

On leaving the South School at the start of the 1940s Alex McKinnon was employed by T & R Graham, lithographic printers. 'I was offered an apprenticeship, but the wage was 7/6d (45p) a week there, while I could get 21/- (£1.10p) in the mills. So after a year with Graham's I decided to make the move to Ferguslie Mills, where I worked in the Turning Shop. In those days all the spools used in the mills were made of wood.

'When I was called up I went into the RAF, where I applied to become a pilot or navigator. They sent

The mills had a fine musical tradition, with both brass and pipe bands. This picture shows one of Ferguslie's Pipe Bands in all their finery.

Photo Courtesy of Old Paisley Society

me to a London college in order to take my education up to Higher standard, but after six months they discovered that they had more students than they needed, so some of us were given the option of becoming air crew, going back to Civvy Street, or becoming Bevan boys and working down the mines.'

Alex chose to become a gunner, flying in Lancaster bombers. When the war ended he was sent to India where he served his final year in Air Traffic Control before being demobbed in 1946.

Hush-hush Job

'Back home, all the mill had to offer me was a job as a machinist in the Twisting Department, where they had introduced a night shift in an attempt to catch up with production after the war. I took it, but I told them that with the extra education I had received while in the RAF I wanted something more challenging.'

Six months later he became a foreman; then followed stints on the Barber Coleman cheese winding machines, working with rotor cones, then with a new German winding machine.

'By that time new synthetic materials were coming in, and there were problems with nylon threads, since they didn't shrink. The laboratory people got onto it and a new American machine was brought in to treat the nylon and enclose it in a cotton core. That was a hush-hush job; Coats was the only company in Britain to try out this new machine and only folk with nametags were allowed to go near it. It caused a lot of interest in the mills.'

Then followed three months in South Africa, where Alex helped to teach local factory workers how to use the new machinery. There should have been stints in Portugal and Italy as well, but by that time the world was changing. The Coats factories in other countries preferred to use their own local workers rather than people from the parent factories in Paisley, and modern work practices had begun to bite. Alex returned to Paisley, where the days of the Ferguslie complex were numbered.

The Pension Fund and Staff Union

After the war he had become involved in the company's pension fund and staff union, and when it was decided to break up the fund into local units he became chairman of the unit covering Ferguslie and Anchor Mills and the Kinning Park depot in Glasgow.

When departments within Ferguslie Mills began to close down, putting employees out of work, Alex, as chairman of the pension fund and staff union, was involved in negotiating redundancy packages for staff.

'One thing we had gained was the right of the employees to opt for a lump sum and a reduced pension if they wished instead of having to take the entire pension as a monthly payment. We tried for years for that, and I was pleased that we managed it before the mill closed.'

Eventually and inevitably, Alex himself was caught up in the redundancies, taking early retirement after putting in 41 and a half years with Coats Vyella.

'And once that happened, I became busier than ever! I was asked to help a group of ladies to form a small choir; I did, and they are still going strong.' The Nightingales sing at functions all over Paisley and beyond, and they are never short of bookings.

Music has always been a part of Alex's life. His father sang in the Paisley Male Voice Choir and an aunt played the piano at the old Alex Cinema in Paisley, and later ran a dance band with her husband. As well as singing in his church choir, then looking after the junior choir, Alex played the bagpipes from the age of 7, and was a member of Anchor Pipe Band.

In 1938 my father decided to buy the chemist's shop at the corner of Ferguslie and Ferguslie Walk in Paisley. Naturally he had to find somewhere to live as at the time we were living in Glasgow, which meant an hour's journey each way every day. By good chance one of the Mill houses in Maxwellton Road, No. 71, was unoccupied at the time; my father was able to rent the house and so my parents, younger brother and myself moved to Paisley.

At that time it was mill policy to use local trades people to supply the mills and so my father was given the job of supplying all first-aid materials to the First Aid Centre. I was given the job of delivering them to the F.A.C. and, in a sense, that was my first encounter with my future employer.

I left school just after the war finished and, as I had not made up my mind as to what I wanted to do career wise, I was called up to serve King and Country for the duration of the emergency, which fortunately was only two years. After demob I still hadn't a clue as to what I was going to do, when a fairly senior member of Mill staff suggested to my mother that I apply to the Coats Head Office in Glasgow as they were looking for young men to train for management to replace staff who had been kept on during the war and were now approaching retiral age.

It Helped To Be A Little Mad!

I applied, was interviewed by a Mr. Ellis at the St. Vincent Street office and accepted, and told to report to the Mile End Mill on a Monday in October 1948.

It had been explained to me at my interview that I would have to start as an ordinary hourly paid worker as Government legislation stated that all promotions must come from within the organisation and by selection tests and interviews. I therefore started in the Reeling Department, which was on the top floor of the mill. This was not a difficult job but it was rather monotonous. It consisted of winding yarn from packages, bobbins or cheeses, into hanks to be used in the Bleaching and Dyeing Departments.

After a few weeks, applications were invited for promotion to the staff. I applied, and after a series of tests and interviews I was once again accepted and transferred to the West Dyeworks on March 14th, 1949 to begin training for dye works management.

As to what it was like in the department, I can't do better than quote a local resident in Seedhill Road who was overheard saying that her husband had been sent into the dyeworks and had told his wife they were all mad in there. It certainly helped to be a little mad!

It is not easy to describe the dyeing process in a short article, and in fact many books have been written on the subject, describing how materials have been coloured since ancient times to the present day. Basically, colouring materials are dissolved in water, generally with the aid of chemicals, and the material is passed through the colour, either mechanically or by hand, until the required shade is obtained. This can be a quite difficult and lengthy process and it is where the skill of the dyer becomes apparent.

The longer it takes to achieve the shade the more expensive it becomes, and so it is the dyer's job to try to have the shade accepted at the initial attempt. This is not easy! In fact, on one occasion when I had been struggling with a difficult shade an old dyer said, 'You should have been a baker, then you could have eaten what you spoiled (or, to use his words, 'whit ye spiled.') It didn't do to be thin-skinned in the Dyeworks.

A Hardy Breed

The work was hard and wet and often cold, especially in winter, as dye baths that had been left overnight could have a covering of ice on them in the morning. However, dyers were a hardy breed in those days and we soon had steam valves opened and the baths heated up to dyeing temperatures. This brought another winter hazard as the steam then formed a mist, which made moving about fun.

There were a considerable variety of machines, all with their own idiosyncrasies, so the dyers had to remember all manner of sequences and processes in dealing with them. Some machines were kept for specific dyeing methods and generally dyers were kept on these machines in the interests of efficiency.

There were three dyeworks in the Paisley Mills, one in Ferguslie and two in Anchor, although formerly there had been two in Ferguslie also. Ferguslie produced mainly sewing threads and the bulk of the black dyeing, and Anchor produced the embroidery threads. At this time, the 1940s and 1950s, the combined dye works must have been producing about 250,000 lbs of thread weekly. A lot of sewing must have been going on to use that amount of thread.

To try to name people I worked with would produce a telephone directory! One of the specialities of the Dyeworks was the use of nicknames, which were always used, and it could be some time before the baptismal name of some dyers was learned. Cork E'e, Tottie Boy, Bomber, Deid Man, Hoolet, Toot, Plum, Doo, Sot, Algerian Joe, Shoogly and College Boy are a few that come to mind.

Seeing the World

Changes were afoot, however, and new fibres were being produced such as Nylon and Terylene, which demanded new machinery and methods. The dye works were gradually changing over to these new fibres and this improved working conditions as the old manhandling of materials was replaced by more up-to-date methods.

At the same time overseas markets were demanding that thread should be made within the marketplace instead of being imported, and so the company started on a huge expansion programme. Once again I was moved on and started on my travels to a number of overseas units.

My first posting was in Germany in 1953 (I think!) to Firma Mez A.G. in Freiburg im Breisgau, a university town near the Black Forest. The plan was that a young German trainee would go to Paisley while I was in Germany. This never happened, for reasons I never learned, but I had a most enjoyable time, although working hard and trying to learn German. At that time Germany was going through a massive rebuilding programme and things were very hard for the workers as there were many shortages of consumer goods. I stayed in digs with a family who looked after me very well and were glad of the extra income.

It was only a short rail journey into Switzerland where as a British visitor it was possible for me to buy coffee, chocolate, cigarettes and other items that were in short supply in Germany. These were greatly appreciated by my landlady and so, with another trainee from Paisley, I made a trip every month to buy these goodies. Strictly speaking it was an offence for us to do this as we had work permits, which meant that we were classed as German citizens as far as imports were concerned. Luckily we were never caught, or we might have ended in Colditz!

The German workers were in many respects very like their opposite numbers in Paisley and I felt at home with them. They also accepted me and included me in any outings or evening entertainments they were having. Many of the men had suffered badly during the war on the Russian front and, in fact, one foreman had only returned from Siberia shortly before I arrived, six years after the end of the war.

A Bit of a Challenge

On completion of my term of training in Freiburg I returned to Paisley via Belgium where I had a crash course in a particular type of Black dyeing which I was to use in Turkey, my next posting. This was a new unit, which was being built on the banks of the Golden Horn in Istanbul. My job was to set up the Bleaching, Mercerising and Dyeing Department, hire and train the workers and get the place up and running. This was a bit of a challenge as Turkish is not the easiest language to learn; however after a couple of years I was on the move again this time to Colombia.

Another country, another language, but things were different now as I had married and had a wife and baby son with me.

The J. & P. Coats sewing thread stand at the Paris Exhibition in 1878.
Photo Courtesy of the Old Paisley Society.

42

The mill was still being built when we arrived, so life was pretty hectic. Fortunately the British staff were all very helpful and the wives soon made my wife welcome and showed her the ropes. This trip lasted about six years and then it was back to Paisley.

Then followed a few more short visits on my own to Mexico, America, Germany and Italy, but most of the time I spent in Anchor, either in the Dyeworks or Research Laboratory.

In the early 70's I was transferred to another Division of the Coats Patons company and ended up in Bolton but working in Bury until I took early retiral.

(Note - Alec's father was one of those killed in May 1941, while on duty in the Woodside First Aid Post.)

 # A Dyers' Diatribe

(From Alec Stewart - Recited at the Midlands Region Annual Dinner)

You'll find in mills throughout the land
A highly skilful select band
Of men, who wait for shouts of ire
From all and sundry -'Send for t'dyer.'

No matter what the trouble be,
Everyone's in unity,
You don't blame tuner, spinner, buyer.
You simply holler -'Send for t'dyer. '

If standing marks the cloth should mar,
One need not look so very far,
Do not the gentle weaver fire,
Better still to -'Send for t'dyer.'

Now if the cloth be stained with grease,
Just mark the ticket 'Dirty Piece'
Then at the perch you broadcast fire.
All together - 'Send for t'dyer.'

If the cutting's rough, or the pile too low,
Say 'The back is grinning through,'
(A deeper shade makes the pile look higher)
So once again it's -'Send for t'dyer.'

If the weft's so weak you've to wind it slack,
Blame your old friend Sulphur Black.
Keep on and on, and be a trier
Sooner or later they'll - 'Send for t'dyer.'

Menders throw around the pieces,
Causing stains and nasty creases,
The perch can't call the lass a liar,
So there's nowt to do but - 'Send for t'dyer.'

When yarns are full of knots and burrs,
The spinner then is heard to curse
And utter threats most rude and dire,
Says 'Can't be MY fault - Send for t'dyer.'

But when things go wrong and you need some aid
In the complex tricky Textile Trade,
If you feel you're really in the mire,
Just relax and -'Send for t'dyer.'

Oh noble men! Oh happy breed!
Yours is a thankless task indeed
If the roof fell in or the mill caught fire,
It's a pound to a pinch, they'd - 'Send for t'dyer.'

But when his earthly span is o'er,
And he stands and waits at the Golden Shore,
He'll hear the call of the Heavenly Choir,
'Bring the best in first - Send for t'dyer!'

Elizabeth (McIntyre) Wilson

On leaving school, Elizabeth McIntyre found work in the Picture House cinema, first as an usher and then as a cashier. 'I was known as "the smiling cashier," but that was when I was young and carefree!'

She was 19 when she decided to apply for a job in the Anchor Mills, where her older sister worked, in 1948. 'The lady interviewing me asked if I would be willing to work shifts, but before I could answer, a gentleman came into the office and said, "I think Elizabeth has had enough of shifts, working late every night at the Picture House." So they sent me to a day job in the Spooling Department.

'It was known as a clean job, but on that first Friday when we stopped early to clean the machines (which happened every Friday) I thought to myself "if this is a clean job, what's a dirty job like?" It was an unpleasant task.

'There were half a dozen of us young girls in Spooling, and I remember one day when we slipped into the toilets for a quick smoke. Someone must have told on us, because we were all called before one of the supervisors. When he asked if we had been smoking I was the only one who admitted to it. The rest of them just kept quiet.

Noisy and Claustrophobic

'When he said that smoking was forbidden in the mills, I spoke up again and said that I had never been told that, and there were no notices to say that we couldn't smoke in the toilets. Because I had been used to working with the public in my cinema job I had a polite way of speaking, and he said that since I had admitted it, no more would be said about the matter.'

Although most of the men and women who worked in the mills quickly got used to the constant clatter and clamour of the machinery, Elizabeth found it more than she could stand. 'It was claustrophobic, too. My nerves just couldn't cope with it and I had to go on the panel. During all my time off, the mill bosses could not have been nicer to me. They sent me a basket of fruit, and every Bank Holiday, when the workers were paid for the day off, I was paid for that day too.'

After being on the panel for almost 10 months Elizabeth had to face the fact that the mills were just not for her. 'When I went to hand in my notice the young man in the offices said that if I ever wanted to come back there would be a job for me. And I had only worked in the place for a total of 4 or 5 weeks.'

Although she only worked in the mills for a short time, Elizabeth has nothing but praise for the treatment she encountered there. 'They were lovely people and the few memories I do have are happy ones.'

 # Archie Haldane

Archie Haldane began his working life at the age of 14, as a messenger boy for the Co-operative before going into Anchor Mills at the age of 15, during the Second World War.

He started, as most lads did, in the dye-works. His first job was in the Making-up Department where the newly dyed yarn arrived in hanks. The hanks were hung up and the lads in the department had to comb through them with poles to separate the strands and remove any foreign bodies. This process was known as 'scutching.'

Because of the war, male employees were called up wen they reached the age of 18, which meant rapid promotion for the younger lads. Archie became an overseer at 17, a job he held until his own turn came to be called up. Each mill department had an overseer (female overseers were known as 'Mistresses') answerable to a foreman, who in turn answered to a sub-manager, who answered to a manager.

After the war Archie worked in the Cotton Mill then finally moved to the Ticketing Department, in the Finishing section, where he was trained as a tenter. The tenter's skill was learned in the mill itself, from the other tenters, and it involved making sure that all the machines were running properly, and resetting them when necessary, so that they could deal with different work.

Every Lad's Ambition

'Being a tenter was every lad's ambition. It wasn't a trade, but it was skilled enough, and some tenters felt that they were better than tradesmen. In the 1950s and 60s, one tenter in the Ticketing Department had five machines under his care.'

When the machines were all set and running smoothly the tenters' lives could be quite peaceful - until the next problem came along. Archie enjoyed working in the Ticketing Department but when he was moved into the Spooling Department he found the work hard. 'The women there were on piecework and if their machines were lying idle it meant that they lost money. So they were always putting pressure on the tenters to get the machines set up and running. Some could be difficult, but others could be very helpful and work with the tenter rather than criticising him.'

 # Margaret (Marshall) Haldane

Margaret Marshall started in the Anchor Mills at the age of 14, as a messenger girl. 'When you first started in the mills they checked your hair for lice and looked at your teeth. It wasn't an enjoyable experience, but it happened to everyone. They were particular about cleanliness.'

She was later transferred to the Examining Department, 'where we examined the cotton to make sure that it was in good condition. After that I became a desk girl in the Reeling Department. Each department on piecework had its own desk girl. Piecework workers were paid for the amount of work they did, which meant that they couldn't afford to take time off and when the tea breaks came in, in the 1940s, most of them drank their tea at their machines.'

Margaret eventually became a tester, checking the strength of the cotton. For a while she worked in Ferguslie Mills, but she preferred Anchor, where she had been from leaving school.

The Examining and Banding Department in the 3rd flat of the Domestic Finishing Mill, 1953.
Photo Courtesy of Old Paisley Society

Dancing in the Corridors

'We worked hard in the mills, but we had a lot of fun too. I remember learning to dance in the corridors, and in the toilets we learned how to pluck our eyebrows and how to pierce each other's ears. I learned to crochet and do Fair Isle knitting there as well.'

As a tester, Margaret was a timeworker, paid by the hour, and unlike the piece-workers, she could organise her workload. 'The cotton was brought to my machine in bogies (wheeled carts) and if I was away for any length of time I would come back to find a row of bogies waiting for me.

'The recreation club at the Anchor Mills was good. In the 40s it cost 2/6d. to join, and there was bowls, badminton, tennis and dancing. On Sma' Shot Day we went off for the day in buses or trains to places like Whitley Bay.'

 # Esther (Durnan) Agnew

Esther Durnan was born in Campbeltown and brought to Paisley by her parents when she was six weeks old. She went into the Anchor Mill on July 15th, 1951, one week after leaving school. She lived at that time in Lacy Street, and her mother, who worked in the Mills bleachwork, didn't want her to go into the mill. "It's not for you," she said. But I was determined, and I never regretted it.'

Esther started in the Balling Department as a 'ball carrier', replacing boxes of thread once the machinists had filled them, and sending the full boxes to an upper floor by the hoist. 'At lunchtimes we fetched the machinists' coats for them so that they could keep the machines running until the last minute. They were on piecework.'

She then went to the Mile End Mill as a 'band former', banding finished embroidery thread, before going into the Dolling Department, still a part of the embroidery section. After that came Synthetic Tube Winding and stints as an examiner, desk worker and a 'shorts girl' (a progress chaser) with the task of making sure that orders went out on time from all departments. After that she went into Production Control.

Esther Agnew in her VAD Uniform, 1950s.
Photo Courtesy of Esther Agnew

Challenging the Foremen

'I was lucky; I enjoyed every job I had. I particularly enjoyed being a shorts girl - if a foreman told me that I wasn't going to get completion of a job when it was needed I would say, "I don't suppose you can manage it," and then they would reach the target just to prove me wrong.'

When she was 22 Esther applied to train as a VAD - a member of the Voluntary Aid Detachment. At that time Anchor and Ferguslie Mills' First Aid rooms each had its own doctor as well as a nursing sister aided by mill workers working as VADs on a shift system. 'Dr Scott and Dr Graham were very good doctors, and I specially remember Margaret O'Brien, one of the nurses. She was a very tall lady and a real character.'

Esther also has fond memories of one of the VAD commandants, Mrs Susan Grant. 'She worked in the Gassing Department at Anchor, and she was a wonderful person. So many of them were.'

Eventually the First Aid rooms in both mills were run by the VADs with a nursing sister based in Anchor Mills to give help and advice when needed.

'Working shifts as we did, we often had to make our own decisions when the sister was off duty, and we managed very well. The First-Aid room had its light moments. I remember measuring a young girl during a medical check-up and telling her that she was 5' 2". "I am not," she argued, "I'm only 5'1". I bumped my head last night and it's the bump that's making me taller."

'Another girl had to get treatment after an accident - she fell off her platform shoes, which were in the fashion at the time. After that, she threw them away.

'I loved being a VAD. I even studied for my degree in chiropody, not that I was particularly interested in chiropody but that way I could learn about anatomy and physiology."

Esther is still involved with the Red Cross movement. A keen singer all her life, she is also part of a Foxbar-based group of entertainers known as The Nightingales, run by a former mill foreman, Alec McKinnon.

Crossing the Great Divide

Esther "crossed the great divide" as one general manager termed it, when she applied for a job as a Records Clerkess in the Personnel Department at Ferguslie. As it happened, the man who interviewed her for the post turned out to have spent holidays with relatives of hers in Campbeltown. After she had moved to Ferguslie Mill a VAD was needed for the First-Aid room there, and so Esther got the job.

Mill V.A.D.s in the 1950s. Esther Agnew is third from left, back row.
Photo Courtesy of Esther Agnew

'The Ferguslie workers were always very down to earth. They called a spade a spade, which suited me. In Anchor Mills the embroiderers thought they were a bit better than anyone else, and at Ferguslie Mills it was the finishers. I have heard, but mind you, I don't know if it's true, that some finishers wore their fur coats to work.'

Esther was the first married woman to be a VAD in the mills; before her time women had to leave when they married. 'One single woman told me, "you can't have a job and a man too." But I did.'

Because she worked in the First-Aid room Esther was one of the last to leave when Ferguslie Mill closed. 'I would have liked to retire from the mills instead of being made redundant as I eventually was, but I loved every minute of my time there, it was like being part of a family. We had some great laughs. We all looked out for each other, and I would say that the mill owners looked after us as well.'

Mothers are usually right, but in Esther's case her mother was wrong when she told her young daughter, 'The mills aren't for you.'

 # May (McArthur) Morrell

May McArthur followed her pals into Ferguslie Mills when she left school, beginning her 40-year stint in 1951, as a Baines runner.

'We worked on the Baines machines in Finishing, on the east side of the mill complex. The machines were operated by hand, and the spooler put the bobbins in, then when the thread had been wound onto them, it was the runner's job to take the bobbins away, ready to be transported to the warehouse.

'I mind once when I was with a crowd of girls who decided to go out for fish and chips during our break. I was on a 2-10 p.m. shift then, with a half hour break at 5 o'clock. We stopped on our way back to talk to some of the boys in the Turning Shop and the foreman, Tommy Kerr, must have spotted us from the window.

'We Were Terrified That Our Mothers Would Find Out!'

'When we finally got back to our own flat he was waiting for us. We got a row, and he wrote down all our names and told us that he was going to give the list to the manager, and we would probably be suspended for being late back. We were all in tears, terrified that our mothers would find out. But nothing happened - I think he just wanted to give us a fright, and he never did pass that list to the manager.'

Later, May became an examiner in the Mechanised Spooling Department. Every single spool that came off the machines had to be checked, and if any faults were found, they were discarded.

'I worked in that department for about five years, then Ferguslie Mills were closed and we were all moved to the Anchor Mills, where I worked with the new American machines that did turret winding. Bill Chittick had been sent to America to see how these machines worked, and when they were installed in Paisley he came back as sub-manager.'

Trained to have Different Skills

During her time in the mills May worked in several departments. 'They liked to have employees with several different skills, so that they could be moved from one department to another, going wherever they were needed. I was a desk girl in the Hank Winding Department, and I also worked as what was known as a shorts girl, which is an office job. In the Hank Winding, we had two sections, SPT, which had English machines that spun big cones for industrial sewing, and PA. I had to learn to be desk girl for both sections so that I could switch from one to the other when needed.'

Desk girls had the task of recording all the materials that came into their department and then checking it out again once it had been processed. Shorts girls made sure that the various jobs in hand were completed within the designated time. 'I mind, before I became a shorts girl myself, we used the call the woman who had that job "Mrs Hurry" because she was always chasing about, following up the jobs that were being done.

Newton Mearns

'The winding department was in the Mile End Mill, and we worked shifts, with a half-hour break. It was continuous working, which meant that when one spooler was on her break, another spooler had to keep two machines going. We had a wee canteen on the 5th floor.'

Then came the closure of Anchor Mills and the move to Newton Mearns, which May didn't like at all. 'It was all on the level, like one big flat, and there were no windows. We had to travel there by bus, and sometimes we were really late getting home, so I decided to take redundancy.'

Like many former millworkers, May says, 'It was hard work, but we got a lot of laughs. And the mills had their traditions; when one of the women retired, her machine was all decorated and so was the area round it. The presents from her workmates were laid out for folk to see, and the manager came to shake hands with her and wish her well.

'May McArthur's got a man!'

'And there were the celebrations when a girl was getting married too, of course. When it was my turn I was dressed up and paraded round the mill and then along the streets with the girls all shouting, 'Hard up, tin can, May McArthur's got a man!'

May belonged to the modern breed of mill girls in that she got the job by filling in a form and being interviewed, and she was able to return to work after her marriage. Before the 2nd World War, employees had to be 'spoken for' by a relative already working in the mills, and once married, female workers could not return to work in the mills.

'I still remember a lot of the people I worked with. When I started as a Baines runner the foreman was Robert McNaught, and then there was Willie Kennedy, and Mr Green, the manager, and the spooling foreman was Alec McLean. Andy Gibson was foreman of Hank Winding, and he used to say to the girls who were had their hair up in rollers, "I hope you keep those rollers in until you get home," because he knew about us doing each other's hair in the toilets.

'I mind one woman who cleaned the toilets - she wouldn't let any of us in when she had just washed the floor in case we marked it.

'Eleanor Morgan (she later became Mrs McNiven) trained me to be a shorts girl, and Mattie Fraser trained me to be a desk girl in Hank Winding. John Lochhead was one of my managers; he was killed in a road accident. At the Mile End Mill, Mary Jardine was one of the spoolers, and Sadie Slack was another; she went abroad for the company. John Leckie was the foreman, and Mr Rowand was the manager. Alec McLean was the spooling foreman and Mattie Fraser taught me how to work at the hank-winding desk. Then there was Ina Fraser - we still meet up every Sunday.'

Ann (Wilson) Smith

Ann Wilson went into the Anchor Mill in 1951, when she left the South School at the age of 15. 'Everyone went into the mills then. All my friends were going in.'

She was sent to the Bleaching Department, where she started work as a "message girl" in the White Warehouse before moving to the Grey Warehouse, so-called because it dealt with the unbleached thread. There, she made tickets to go on the bags holding the hanks of thread.

'I think I earned about £3 a week in those days. At first, part of my job as the youngest and newest in the department included cleaning the manager's and under-manager's offices, and the bleaching office, and taking mail to and from other departments. I enjoyed that. When a new batch of workers came into the department, the youngest of them took those jobs over from me.

Piecework Made the most Money

'The actual bleaching process was done by men, and the people on piecework made the most money. After the hanks were bleached they were put into big stoves to be dried. For a while I worked with the stoves. The hanks had been tied together, like link sausages. Before being put into the stoves the hanks were separated, then eight hanks at a time were put onto a pole for drying. After that, they were made up in bundles of four hanks each, then went into the White Warehouse, where they were bundled and bagged.'

Ann worked in the Bleaching Department for five years before leaving to marry and raise a family. 'I loved working there. I loved the people I worked with, they were great. Our manager was Richard Speirs, a bowler-hat type. We didn't have much to do with him, but he would never ignore any of the people in his department. He was a lovely man and so was the under-manager, Stuart Hutchison. I knew him better because we had more to do with him.

'We Had Great Times'

Then there were the foremen - John Wilson in the White Warehouse, Archie Campbell in Bleaching, and Willie Adams in the Grey Warehouse. They were all good to work with.'

A mill football team, possibly pictured in the 1940s. Details unknown, but the Paisley Thread Mill museum would like to hear from anyone who can identify the team, the year and any of the players.
Photo Courtesy of the Old Paisley Society.

A crepe paper bonnet, streamers and balloons - workmates help a bride-to-be from Anchor Mills to celebrate her forthcoming marriage.
Photo Courtesy of the Old Paisley Society.

Ann also has happy memories of her own colleagues, among them Morag Kennedy, Jean White, her partner when she worked at the stoves, Georgie Reid, the desk girl in the Grey Warehouse, who, sadly, was killed in a car accident; Lottie Cairns, Barbara Hastings, Margaret Thomson and Isobel McSorland.

'I moved to Renfrew when I married, so I lost touch with all of them. But we had great times together in the Anchor Mills.'

 ## Betty (Charnock) Devaney

'My sister put my name forward when I was 15 and I went for an interview with Personnel at the Weighhouse in the Anchor Mill - that was in 1953. I did all the exams and when they tested my eyes they found that I needed glasses, so I never got into the Embroidery section.

'I got started at the Spool Examining in the 3rd flat for a while, and then I was moved to the 4th flat as post girl. I went out with the mail to the dye works and the Mile End Mill.

'I didn't have a good boss. He used to send me out with the next day's orders ten minutes before closing time. One night I had to refuse to go, and I never slept that night for worrying, it was like going before the hangman. A woman asked me if I was in the union, so I joined straight away and I was never sent out ten minutes before closing time again.

'I then went to Quality Control, as assistant to Gerry, a Quality Controller. I had to watch out for broken yarn, and I'd help out with dissecting the wastage to see what most of the problems were. All in all, I was quite happy there.

'There were girls who did all sorts of things for each other. You could get your hair done, your eyebrows plucked, or your ears pierced with a tattie and a needle. I was on shifts 6a.m. to 2 p.m. and 2 p.m. to 10 p.m. I loved the 2 to 10 shift, I could have gone on with that shift forever if they had let me.

The Convalescent Home built at West Kilbride by the Coats family for their employees is now used as a community centre

'I used to put my hair into curlers, and then when I finished work I would comb my hair out and then go to meet my boyfriend John. We would go for a walk and a winch, and then I went home to bed - sometimes I had a wee cycle round first - and then if I was on the early shift I would get up at 5.00 a.m. the next morning and go to work looking a mess.

Sweeties on a Friday

'I stayed in George Street then, down at the Causeyside Street end, and at 5.30 in the morning I met up with a friend who stayed in Johnston Street, and we walked to work together.

'I mind that I hated the winter because we used to get pelted with snowballs from some boys when we went past them. They fairly battered us with snowballs! In those days I was young and easy embarrassed, and I hated going in to work with my hair all wet and straight from the snowballs.

'I loved a Friday when they stopped the machines early for cleaning and we all brought in sweeties. We used to gorge ourselves.

'When I was 15 I had my appendix out and after that I was sent to the Coats Convalescent Home in West Kilbride for two weeks. We all paid a few pence from our wages to keep that Home going. I went there on my own - quite a thought at my age, in those days - but while I was there I met up with people and had a good time.

'In the 3rd floor flats where I worked there was a women called Margaret Brown, she was German, her and I just seemed to hit it off. We called each other names - she would call me "puddin'" and I used to say, "At least I'm not a foreigner." We had a good laugh. Margaret was a great pieceworker. She used to keep up to 6 machines going at the one time. The number of machines you worked depended on the type of yarn. You usually had three or four machines, but never just one.

'As the spools got filled up with thread, they came along in a chain mechanism thing. There were 3 or 4 runners in front of me and these filled up quickly. If you let them overflow the spools went all over the place and that was bad, because it was good clean thread.

Knots or Breakages

'I used to use this tool like a rake with a small handle. The 12 or 14 spikes on it corresponded with the holes in the spools. It meant that I could examine 12 or 14 spools at a time, looking for knots or breakages. If it was just a little cut it could be passed to another table and rectified, but if the thread was knotted, it was scrapped. You always hoped that you wouldn't have a lot of scrap because then your lap bag would be full.

'The spools were then packed into a large tray that held a gross at a time. When the tray was filled, a tenter took it away and I started filling another tray.

'I left the mill when I was 21 to get married, then went back, then left again when I was expecting my twin boys. That was in 1959. When the boys were two or three years old the training I had got in the mills meant that I was taken on at the hank winding at McCallum's in Abercorn Street, where I worked in the evenings.'

 # Catherine (Haughey) Stevenson

'My first memory of J. & P. Coats was going for an interview in October 1953 to the admin. building, a small building facing the main street.

'Two other people were waiting and a third person was being interviewed. These three people eventually went out and then a lady came out of the office carrying an application form, looked round the waiting room and then went back into the office. She did this twice and on the third time she looked at the form, looked at me, and asked if I was Catherine Haughey. I was very small for my age and I wore a big ribbon in my hair. I certainly did not look 15 years old.

'I was taken on, and started in the Packing Department. But I was too small to reach the table, and had to stand on a box, so then I was put on to Trimming and Banding. Jock Lang was my foreman. For the first (I think) six weeks you were paid a basic £1.10/- (150 pence) per week, and then you went onto piecework.

'Being immature and not very streetwise, I was taken in many times by some of the other people working on the line. They used to call me down to talk to them, and while chatting I would be trimming and banding their "parcels" along with them. (A parcel was a tray of thread that was sent along a conveyor belt each time the operator pressed a button).

'I thought I was just popular'

'I was very quick at the job, but in those early days I thought that I was popular for myself, not for how fast I could work.

'After six months, when I was only earning around two pounds while the others were earning £5 and more, my mother found out what was going on from our neighbour, whose daughter worked "on the line" and was one of the people who kept calling me down to talk to her - and help her at the same time.

'Another thing some of the machinists did was to change the numbers on the "parcels". There was good thread and bad thread, with "glassy" thread being a menace to work with. Your number was in the tray, and sometimes people who had a bad lot of thread coming up the line would swap numbers with a good parcel.

'Each Friday lunchtime it was the tradition to go over to the sweet shop and buy sweets, usually two ounces of three or four different kinds, and share them out back at the flat. I also used to buy the new *Musical Express* there each week.

'A great memory I have is going back to our No. 2 flat via the bobbin shop after lunch time   I can still remember the smell of the newly turned bobbins - and there was quite a bit of bit of talent there, among the young apprentices. We did enjoy the wolf whistles from them.

'My uncle Hugh Smith worked in the bobbin shop for years, training apprentices.

'Once during stocktaking a few regulars and myself were sent up to a box room at No. 1 Mill; it was called the Crystal Palace as it was like a big attic with a bay window. I don't know how many boxes we counted but it was great fun as there was no supervisor - a shame the job only lasted a week.

'A Wonder Nobody was Injured'

'When it was time to go home there was always an air of excitement as we waited, crushed against the giant gates, for the whistle to blow. It's a wonder no one was ever injured.

'On Friday afternoons all machines were turned off and everyone had to clean up their area, then we would collect our clean overalls for the following week. It was popular to go to work on Fridays with rollers in your hair, I guess it was all part of the lead up to the weekend.

'I worked for Coats for 13 months and during that time I made many friends and had lots of good times. I left in November 1954 because after nine months you had to go on to shift work - 6 until 2 and 2 until 10, and I did not like shifts.

'My next job was at the Seedhill Finishing Company, where they made Vyella and Clydella. We were a well-dressed Haughey family then! But that's another story.'

Note - *Catherine Stevenson, nee Catherine Haughey, now lives in Australia, and has put her passion for sewing and for lace and fine materials to good use.*
'I have always felt a need to sew, and now I spend most of my time sewing. Baby clothes are my specialty; I don't make a living from them, as I like to give them to people who are in the position that my Mum was in when she had a large family and very little money to buy pretty clothes for us.

'Just now (early 2002) I am making baby clothes for refugees who have come from Iran and Iraq by boat and have been put straight into a detention centre, where there are 800 men, women and children in total. They have a long wait for their refugee status to be processed.'

On a visit to Paisley in 2001, Catherine started chatting to a man at the next table in the Sma' Shot Cottages tearoom. After about ten minutes she discovered that she was talking to Jock Lang, who used to be her foreman in Ferguslie Mills.

Helen (Haughey) Mitchell

'It was 1953-54 and in the scheme of J. & P. Coat's mill lassies, we were considered privileged because we worked in Number 1 Mill on the Barber Colman machines. These monsters had been recently imported from America and it was during my time there that the piecework rates were established. It was a noisy but clean environment.

'The workers were mainly young girls. There was Fay (Moore) Ward, Ellen (Fergus) Farmer, Mary Todd and a big Irish girl called Mary McLaughlin. This Mary worked so hard she put the rest of us to shame. She was saving up to bring her parents and siblings over from Ireland. Ronnie Leach, the foreman, used to say he'd put a nosebag round her neck because she worked like a horse.

'Ronnie was really good looking and always smiling. I think we were all secretly in love with him but another lassie won his heart. I wonder where they are now? There was an older woman in our flat, Mrs Farrell, and she used to give us advice about how to catch a boy friend. That was a main topic for discussion in those days. We never mentioned long term plans, or careers, or travel. The only thing that mattered was getting enough money to buy the latest clothes from Kendall's and still have the price of the Templars or Johnstone Town Hall dancing left.

Happy and Irresponsible

'My 'mill lassie' days were happy and irresponsible. If we needed a break from the noisy machines we'd put an arm up to the spinning "cheeses", get a friction burn and spend the next hour or so in the mill medical centre. These were the days before Health and Safety measures were a big issue for employers.

'Five minutes before the end of each shift there was a "prepare to stop" siren. Then at the final signal hundreds (perhaps it was thousands!) of women would rush for the main gate. There was a time clock there and we each had to find our card and thump it into the clock slot. I can still hear the clang of that clock that signalled freedom! We

Helen Mitchell's graduation in Australia, 2001. Pictured with Helen are (left to right) sisters Anne, Pat, Frances, Catherine Stevenson (also in this book) and Evelyn.
Photo Courtesy of Helen Mitchell

would then rush to the nearest bus stop, still blethering away to whoever was nearest. Another shift was over.'

Helen moved from Canada and then to Australia, where she lives in Adelaide, quite near to her mother and her sister Catherine, both featured in this book.

'This year (1998), I had a wonderful journey back to Paisley and it gave me great joy and pleasure to meet up with friends from those heady days and to see them all so well and happy.

Marjory (Wilson) Cairney

Paisley-born Marjory went to work in the Anchor Mills after leaving school at the age of sixteen. 'That's where everyone went then (in the 1950s) and I had an aunt who worked in the Mills.'

She was started in the PA Winding, a small building up next to the dye works. 'A woman called Betty McFadyen taught me how to use the machine, and after a week I was able to work on my own. I loved it there, but later, they moved me to the Mile End Mill, where we worked with silk threads.

'The trouble with the silk threads was that they kept breaking. We were on piecework, and this meant that every time we stopped to mend the thread we lost wages. Finally I complained about this, and when nobody did anything about it I decided to leave.

'Amazing the way you keep meeting folk'

'I was in the Anchor Mills for three or four years, and that was the only problem I had. They looked after you well. I remember once when I dropped one of the big bobbins onto my toe, I was hurried off to the First-Aid room at once to be seen to.

'It's amazing how once you have worked in the Mills you keep meeting up with people who knew you then. When I worked there I used to go out for my dinner with another machinist, Angela Jenkins. Sometimes we went out and bought something to eat, and sometimes we went to Angela's house in Hunterhill. I had never been in Hunterhill before, but my mother moved there years later and when I visited her, a woman living opposite her, Mrs O'Malley, remembered me from the times I had been there with Angela.

'In spite of leaving over a grievance, I loved working in the mills.'

 # Maisie (Mushet) Hamilton

In the 1950s Maisie Mushet was what the Paisley mill workers called a 'maiden lady buddy', and after her marriage she remained a 'lady buddy' - the mill term for women who always wore hats, and were scandalised when the Queen was first photographed wearing a headscarf.

Maisie began her career with Coats as a sweeper in the Finishing Department, and then when she was in her mid-thirties she started travelling the world in the service of the far-flung Coats Empire.

Once she had been picked to go abroad for the mills, Maisie spent two years learning about the workings of every department before setting off in 1959 to Turkey, where she spent 10 months training the local workforce in a new Coats mill. During that 10 months she lost a lot of weight. 'They didn't cook our sort of food.' But before she left for Colombia, every worker in the Turkish mill knew how to say, 'Good morning, Miss Maisie, how are you?'

She has seen bullfights (which she loved) and cockfights (which she hated) and communal circumcisions. She can count in Turkish and converse in Spanish.

'The public were the worst people to deal with.'

Colombia was too primitive for her liking - the people were very poor and to Maisie's mind the women had disgraceful morals. She was then posted to Peru, where the factory girls used to say 'Poor Miss Maisie,' because she wasn't married. Lima has many happy memories for Maisie - the area held a sizeable international expatriate community, and Maisie, who became a member of the Lima Cricket

Club, lived at a *pension* 'run by a proper lady.'

In 1964 Maisie returned to Scotland and married, but she continued to work in the Paisley mill for the next ten years, finally leaving to take up a job in a corset shop. It was a move she regretted. 'The public were the worst people to deal with.'

Maisie is proud of the years when she worked for Coats, both at home and abroad. The mills, she says, were good to their workers. 'Though in a sense it wasn't fair what they did to me. All the men who went abroad ended up as managers, but because I knew all the different departments I got sent to Quality Control.'

When she started work there were no unions in the mill. 'There was no need for them. But later, as they mechanised more and more of the production, trying to extract every last penny, the unions found it easier to recruit.'

'I didn't take anything to do with them, even when I left. In my opinion the mills had always been fair to the workers. I saw a lot of the world, and I certainly had to work hard, but I really did enjoy my time with the firm. It was a chance in a lifetime.'

 # Agnes McLean

Agnes McLean was born in Barshaw Hospital and lived in Kilnside Road until she was nine years old, when her parents moved to Bank Street. Agnes was the fourth generation of her family to live in the Bank Street flat.

After being educated at the East School and Camphill School - 'all those buildings are gone now,' - she started work in Galbraith's Store in Cotton Street. When she was 16 years of age her father died suddenly, and Agnes moved from Galbraith's to the Anchor Mill because she could earn more money as a mill worker.

It was early in the 1950s, and machinery in the Ticketing Department in the Domestic Finishing Mill was in the process of becoming mechanised. Agnes started work on one of the older machines, moving later to a more modern machine. 'I was with a good team, we had a lot of laughs.'

After seven years in Ticketing, she moved for a short time to the dye works, and then went back to Ticketing, since by then most of the domestic thread work was being done abroad. Agnes worked as a machine operator on cop banding, putting the cellophane wrapping on small cops. Each team consisted of a boxer, a machinist and a labeller.

An Enjoyable Job

Agnes eventually took on the task of teaching newcomers, earning extra payment for her teaching duties, and then she was moved to Dispatches, where all the finished work was sent off to the central warehouse at Kinning Park.

'We marked up the production in the pay books and I was also taught how to do the special orders. I ended up working in the basement on the "hot line dispatches". This was work that had to be sent out very quickly. We had a three-day turnaround, and the van driver, Tom Wilson, and I were more or less left to work on our own. I enjoyed that job - I remember that there was a sink behind where I worked, and sometimes on a Saturday morning when the work was done Tom would give his wee West Highland terrier a bath in it.'

The year-long miners' strike in 1984/85 put an end to the 'hot line' duties and Agnes returned to Dispatch on the 6th floor flat. 'I did week and week about with someone else on SDS - the special delivery service - and when she left, I took over and did it full time.'

When personnel from Kinning Park were brought into the mill to deal with the special deliveries,

19th century mill workers leaving Anchor Mills at the end of a shift. Note the long skirts and shawls.
Photo Courtesy of the Old Paisley Society.

Workers in Ferguslie No. 1 Spinning Mill, pictured in 1976.
Photo Courtesy of the Old Paisley Society.

Agnes went onto working an adapted Fuji machine, originally designed to wrap packets of biscuits. When the Anchor Mill finally closed down she moved to the mill at Newton Mearns until she was made redundant in 1993.

A hard-working member of the Old Paisley Society, Agnes has also been active in the Paisley Development Society since its beginnings, and has been involved in the process of helping to set up the Paisley Thread Mill Museum to commemorate the mills where she and so many other local lassies spent their working lives.

Ann (Rutherford) Shaw

Ann Shaw, then Anna Rutherford, began working in the examining room at Ferguslie's Old Mill in 1955. 'I filled poles with hanks of thread which were then examined by Jean Davis for faults or flaws. When they had been checked I bundled the hanks together and refilled the poles.

'At that time we didn't have a canteen, so during tea breaks we sat on the bundles of thread to drink our tea, which was brought round the various departments. I was very happy in my job.'

Ann's father, James Rutherford, started work in the Ferguslie dye-works at the age of 14, and stayed there for most of his working life, apart from a four-year stint in the Army. 'He worked shifts, 6 a.m. until 2 p.m., and 2 p.m. until 10 p.m., ' Ann remembers, 'and he cycled to and from work every day. When the Ferguslie Mills closed down he was transferred to the Anchor Mills, where he remained until he retired at the age of 65. He never liked Anchor as much as Ferguslie.'

Ann still remembers quite a few of the people she worked with. 'Apart from Jean Davis, there was Jimmy Howe, the General Manager, and the foreman and forewoman, Bertie Mitchell and Helen Blakely.

'Isa Coates and Nan Pettigrew were in my department as well, and Martha Murphy was a cleaner there, and also a personal friend of my family.'

Ann left the mills in 1958, when she married and moved to Portrush in County Antrim.

Alistair Quail

Between 1956 and 1966 Alistair Quail worked as a tenter on the 5th flat of No. 8 Mill, Ferguslie. 'It was a family affair - my four sisters and my brother all worked in Ferguslie Mills, and my mother was there too, as a supervisory cleaner. One of my sisters, May, worked in the mill for 31 years.

'My job was very hard work indeed. We had about 40 women to keep going in work. They did piecework but we worked for an ordinary wage. This meant that these women earned half of my wages again on top of what I earned, which I felt was very unfair.

'They were quite a good bunch of women but you couldn't have jokes or anything with them as they were too busy trying to make money. We were on shift work - 6 a.m. to 2 p.m., and 2 p.m. to 10 p.m. - six days a week. I think the only thing I could say about working in the mill was, when you started you really thought you had a job for life but as I said, the wages weren't great for men.

Not so Funny!

'There was one incident, which I thought was funny at the time. I was pushing a load of yarn and went over on my ankle. The foreman sent me over to the rest room and the nursing sister there treated my ankle with a sunray lamp and then sent me back to work.

'The pain got worse and by the time I went home for lunch I was in agony. When I told my wife how sore it was, she said, "When you go back to work, tell them." So I walked back to the mill, but by the time I got to the gate I couldn't move another inch and two men had to help me to the rest room. The Sister arranged for a car to take me to the RAI, where my ankle was X-rayed. It turned out that I had pulled ligaments and I was in plaster for six weeks.

The Harder you Worked, the Less you Got

'The mill was a funny place to work; when you worked for a certain length of time in one place, you were then put on to a waiting list for a better job with more wages. The funny thing is the harder you worked the less wages you got.

'I applied for a job as a driver, passed the test and got the job. The Transport Manager was a Mr North. I can't say that I enjoyed working for him. One day I was sent to Nethercraigs to collect a load of yarn. It was packed in big baskets which I had to load on to the lorry, and when I got back Mr North said I had been away too long. He said, "Jimmy Scolland took half the time yesterday."

'I said, "But Jimmy had half the load that I had today, and if you want, you can send Jimmy every day.' He was not very happy. After that I decided to look for another job.'

 # June (Shaw) Quail

June Shaw was 15 when she went into the Anchor Mills, working in the Domestic Finishing Mill. And she was only 16 when she had her first, and most serious, brush with authority. She was working at a machine that put the cellophane wrapping on reels of thread and the supervisor asked her to work into her tea break to complete the gross.

'I did it, but when the break was over he expected me to start work at the same time as everyone else. When I said that I was due the extra time I'd worked there was a right row. The foreman, sub-manager and manager were all called and I told them that my dad said right's right and wrong's wrong, and it was wrong to refuse me the five minutes I had worked into my break.'

Eventually her father was summoned from the Ferguslie Mills. He made June apologise to everyone and she was suspended for three days. 'That supervisor destroyed something in me. The Paisley people were always rebels, but that guy killed the fire in me.'

Despite the unfair punishment June enjoyed her time as a mill girl. 'You were never lonely. Wherever you went you always met someone who worked there as well. You could go on your own to any one of Paisley's dance halls - the Templars or the Town Hall or the Anchor Rec or the Big Co. - and you'd find someone to pal up with. In the queue for the pictures you would see somebody you knew and join in with them.'

The Ear-piercing That Went Wrong

The toilets were a focal point in the mill girls' day. 'That's where you got all the gossip. Men couldn't go into the female toilets so the foreman used to tell a female worker to go in, and say, "If there's more than two in there, send somebody out." Girls used to get their hair cut in the toilets, and their tealeaves read and their ears pierced with a long needle and a bar of soap to hold behind the earlobe. One time the girl doing the piercing missed the mark and jabbed a bystander in the neck. She pierced her carotid artery and the blood was spurting like a fountain."

A marriage made in the Paisley Mills - June Shaw and Alistair Quail, a tenter in Anchor Mills, pictured on their wedding day.
Photo Courtesy of June (Shaw) Quail

June had a screaming fit at sight of all the blood. She had to be helped over to the First Aid room, followed by the other girl, who had her hand pressed to her neck to stem the bleeding. When they reached the First Aid room the nurse hurried to help June, who was still hysterical, and it was a moment or two before she identified the real emergency.

Mill girls have always loved dancing. 'Girls on the six-to-two shift used to wear their hair in curlers under turbans, so that they could go out to the dancing as soon as the afternoon shift was over. They were called the mill hairies.'

Another custom that endured through generations was 'cleeking' - walking to and from the mills tightly linked arm in arm. When the hooter went at the end of the day, rows and rows of mill lassies swept along the street, arms linked, 'and woe betide anyone who got in the road!'

The mills offered social and recreational activities, but it was the 1950s and June and her pals had their own interests. 'We organised our own trips to Blackpool and other places, and we wore waspy belts and sticky-out skirts and black raincoats with gold inside. You tied the belt tight and turned the collar up, and walked with a bit of a swagger because you were a mill worker.'

Belting out pop songs

The women looked after each other, and on occasion food parcels were made up for those who weren't able to work. June recalls working alongside a woman who was the sole breadwinner for her mother and two brothers. 'She was a slow worker - as we would say, the meter was empty and the lights weren't in.' So June and her pal Cathy set to and made up the extra work for their slower colleague.

Memories include belting out pop songs over the thunder of the machines and bribing the tenters with biscuits so they'd come quickly if your machine broke down. Being pushed round the mill in a bogey before you got married, and the pandemonium when a mouse was spotted running through the flat.

'Nobody ever made trouble at work. The money was better in the mills than anywhere else and you never wanted to put a foot wrong in case you got into bother. There was good and bad in the mills. If it hadn't been for them, Paisley wouldn't have prospered the way it did. I don't think there was a street in the town without at least one mill-worker living in it. The owners were good to their workers in a way, with the first-aid classes and the sports facilities and the nursing homes, but in other ways they weren't so good.'

Future Mill employees June Shaw (left) and Muriel Smith.
Photo Courtesy of June (Shaw) Quail

60

She has bad memories of the way her father was treated, losing out on his redundancy money after working in the mills for 46 years just because his service had been interrupted by the war. And she remembers the phone call that came a few days after his death, telling her mother not to lift his pension because he hadn't lived out the full week.

June worked in the mills between 1952 and 1955. 'Not a long time, but I shoved a lifetime into those three years. All in all, I loved it.'

 # Ellen (Fergus) Farmer

Like thousands of girls before her, Ellen Fergus went from school at the age of 15, to Ferguslie Mill.

'After passing a few tests for reading and writing and getting a check-up at the Medical Centre I was started in the Old Mill, being taught by an older, experienced woman how to work a Barber Colman Winder. It was hard work and the place was noisy and a bit scary at first, but the older women were very patient with the new girls and friendly too - though that didn't stop them sending me out to the serviceman for a bucket of steam during my first week!'

Ellen recalls passing the old canal on the way to the canteen for her first dinner break. 'It was full of fish. The mill girls made pets of them and fed them, and the fish were so tame that they used to watch for people passing, and almost jump out of the water to grab the food. The canteen itself was large and modern, with polished wood floors and a stage at the back. At one end French windows led out to a garden. It wasn't a bad place to eat your lunch after a busy morning, and the meals were cheap because they were subsidised by Coats.

'We used to have great nights out - and not a drop of alcohol!' Ellen Farmer (right) on a mill outing to Butlins of Ayr, with pals Moira Hampsey (centre) and Agnes McCrudden (left).
Photo Courtesy of Ellen Farmer

Hard Work and Long Hours

'My first week's wage was £3.12/6d (£3.65p), a good wage for a young girl in these days, but I earned it because the work was hard and the hours, 7.30 in the morning till 5.30 in the afternoon, were long.'

In true mill girl tradition, Ellen knew how to enjoy herself in her free time. 'Paisley had eight picture houses and there was dancing at many of the halls in Paisley. Two of the most popular dancehalls were Paisley Town Hall and the New Templars Hall. They both sold soft drinks only, or tea and coffee. It wasn't the done thing then for women to go into pubs.

'Because we earned good money we could all afford to live up to our reputation as the best dressed women in the West of Scotland. For holidays we headed for Saltcoats and Ayr and other coastal towns, but some of the mill girls saved up and went to exotic places like Ostend.

Perfume Machines

'We had rows of spotless clean toilets with showers and perfume machines on the wall. You paid for a spray of perfume, and Black Rose was my favourite. If we brought our own towels we could have showers before or after our shifts.

' I even had my ears pierced in the toilet by one of the girls. One ear was done at the first tea break and the other at the second. I was scared stiff but I went ahead because I didn't want to look a coward. We even learned how to do the latest dance steps in the toilets, but that was easy because the room was big and it had polished wooden floors.'

At 16 years of age Ellen went onto shift work, 6am to 2pm., and 2pm to 10pm. 'I also went onto piecework, which meant that we were paid for the amount of work we did. If we worked hard enough we could double our wages, but girls of my age were more interested in what we did in our spare time. While we gossiped during the working day about where we were going that night, the married women worked non-stop to make money for their families. Some of them didn't even take their tea breaks.'

It was quite common for a group of the younger women to head for one of the town's cinemas right after their shift ended, in order to keep up with the latest releases. Sometimes film stars visited the mills when they were in Paisley to promote a film at one of the local picture halls.

The Pay was Rubbish!

'I remember when we got a visit from Lana Morris, who appeared in some of the Norman Wisdom films, and also Sylvia Sims. We were really impressed with their mink coats and high-heeled shoes and beautiful dresses and lovely long eyelashes. It was only years later that I realised the eyelashes were false.'

A few years after Ellen started in the mill her mother decided that she should get a better job with more prospects. 'So I went to work in a fruit shop, and I hated it because the pay was rubbish and I was treated like a slave. After six months I tried working in Galbraiths Bakery in Govan but the working conditions were awful and I was glad to get back to the mill and to my friends there.

'It was hard work in the mills, make no mistake about that, but it was rewarding and the mill girls were a credit to the town. Many of them left the mills to go to other jobs and with the experience they had gathered they moved onward and upwards. I count myself lucky to have such memories, and to have many good friends to this day that I met while working in the mill.'

Note - Ellen, President of the Old Paisley Society and a keen local historian, was awarded the MBE in 1998 for her services to Paisley and to the Old Paisley Society.

Margaret McFadden worked in both Ferguslie and Anchor Mills, starting in Ferguslie straight from school, when she was 15 years of age. That was during the 1950s.

'I was put into the Twisting Department as a doffer I worked on a doffing machine, which transferred the thread from reels to large bobbins. The bobbins were then put into a box and taken to Examining. We were trained by older workers, usually spinster ladies - very prim and proper, but lovely ladies. I was trained by Jessie Burgess. You couldn't go onto piecework until you were 16 years old, and then you started working the two-shift system. With piecework, the harder you worked, the more you were paid. I remember Mary Jordan from that time, and Hamish McCall was our foreman.'

Not long after Margaret started work there was a strike in the mill. The younger girls, too young to join the Union, had to keep on working, and passing through the picket lines, past their striking colleagues, was a frightening experience.

'I was petrified because they were hissing and spitting as us. I agreed with the way they felt, and their reason for striking, and I knew that it wasn't a personal thing with them, but it was very unpleasant.'

Clyde Valley Stompers

Fortunately, that unhappy memory was an isolated incident, and Margaret still looks back with pleasure on her time at Ferguslie, such as running home to present her mother with the first five-pound note she had ever earned, when she became a piece worker.

'I ran all the way home because I didn't

A typical mill flat in the 1930s, apart from the bunting, which marks a special occasion. In this flat, the women had to stand at their machines all day.
Photo Courtesy of Old Paisley Society

want to break that note for my bus fare. I wanted to give it to her.' And there were the nights out with the pals she made in the mill. 'I mind when the Clyde Valley Stompers played at dances in Paisley Town Hall. We always seemed to be on the late shift when they were in Paisley, and it was a rush for us to get washed and changed and get our hair done, then we had to run like hell to get into the dancing.'

Fridays were special. A pieceworker could make up a full weeks' wages by Thursday night, and younger workers, with no families to worry about, were often content to leave it at that. 'On Fridays we took in sweeties; half a pound each, and we all bought different sweets so that we could pass them round. And we sang songs above the noise of the machines. My job on a Friday was to pluck the lassies' eyebrows for the Saturday night dancing. Someone else would run my machine for me while I was doing it; the foreman was good, he didn't mind as long as the work was done. Another girl dyed and bleached hair, and someone else set the lassies' hair, using different-sized tubes from the Tube Winding. You could never do that sort of thing nowadays.'

Hats, Gloves and Facecloths

After three or four years at Ferguslie Mills, Margaret moved to the Anchor Mill. 'They sent me to the Embroidery, and oh, I didn't like it at all! The women who worked there came to their work wearing hats and gloves, and they were so posh they even had their own face cloths. Don't get me wrong, they were really nice people, but a bit sedate. It just wasn't for me. I kept asking to be moved.'

Finally Margaret got her move - to the Gassing Department, where the thread was passed at speed through machines that burned off stray wisps to make it suitable for sewing. 'It was one of the heaviest and dirtiest jobs you could get in the mills - and I loved it. Again, many of the other women were older than me and they had been there for years. They had learned to tolerate the work, but I liked it from the first day I started there.'

When she was saving to get married Margaret left the mills and went to work at Grant's whisky bond, for more money without shifts. But she soon returned to the mill.

'I was married from the mills in 1962. I got the usual reception from the other women - my coat was done up with crepe, and I got a hat, and then I was paraded around in a pram. And there was a chanty filled with salt and wee dolls. I got a nice ginger jar as a wedding present - I still have it - and they passed round a sheet for me. It went round the two shifts and £100 was collected. That was a lot of money in those days.

'I liked working in both the mills, Ferguslie and Anchor. It's sad to think that these days are over, but I'm glad that the former workers' memories are being collected.

'After all, in those days Paisley was the mills, and the mills were Paisley.'

 # Sheena (Millar) McKee

Sheena Millar started work in Anchor Mills in the mid-1960s when she left Camphill School at the age of 15. 'My mother worked in the Ticketing Department, and I just followed her into the mills. I worked in Production Control as a stock control clerkess. My boss at that time was Gordon Mitchell, he was a good boss to have.'

Sheena enjoyed her job, but when she got married two years later, aged 17, she had to give the job up. 'You could go on working in the mills themselves after you were married, but at that time you could not go on working in the offices.'

Part of her job entailed going over to the Colour Store regularly, and when Jack Brodie, a foreman in the store, heard that she was going to have to leave Production Control, he suggested that she could work for him instead. 'He was a lovely man.'

The job was much the same as her work in Production Control - keeping stock records - and Sheena stayed in the Colour Store for a further two years before giving up work to start a family.

'My mother was still working in Ticketing, and I used to take the kids to the mill gate at lunchtime to see her. That gave me the chance to meet up with the other women coming out of the mill for their break. And I used to meet up with some of them in Cardosi's in Causeyside Street for a coffee. I have some very happy memories of my time in the Anchor Mills. I made good friends there, like Rena McGlashan, who worked in the counting house, and Helen Thomson and Betty Crighton.'

In the mid-1990s Sheena's husband, a demolition contractor, took on the job of pulling down some of the Anchor Mill buildings.

Margaret (Millar) McKean

Margaret Millar went into Anchor Mill in the 1960s, straight from school. She followed in the footsteps of her mother and older sister, both already working in the mill.

'I worked on the sixth floor of the Mile End Mill, in the Balling Department as a desk girl. The machinists were on piecework and worked in teams of two, with one operating the machine that balled the crochet thread, and the other boxing the completed balls. It was my job to keep a record of the department's work output.

'Because the women were on piecework with their wages dependent on what they produced, there was pressure on them all the time to keep the work going. It got worse after someone went to South Africa and saw machinery there that produced the crochet balls automatically. The South African machinery only needed one person to do the work that two were doing in Paisley, and eventually this machinery was installed at the Anchor Mills.'

The Twilight Shift

Margaret had been in the mills for four years when she got married, and continued to work until her daughter was born. When the little girl was three or four years old the mills brought in 'twilight shifts', and Margaret's mother, who worked in the Ticketing Department, suggested that she and Drina Brown, the good friend she had made during her time in the mills, should apply.

'So we did, and we were both taken on. It was great. It meant that I was back among a crowd again, and earning some money. I went back to my old job as a desk girl in the Balling Department, but it was embroidery wools more than crochet thread by then. I enjoyed working in the mills, something different happened every day and we had a lot of good laughs. Not like nowadays, when people go to work all straight-faced and come home straight-faced.'

Margaret worked on the twilight shift until 1982, when she and her family emigrated to South Africa.

 # Sadie Mains

Sadie worked as a cone winder in Ferguslie for two years during the 1960s, full time in Mill 1 at first, then on the twilight shift after her family came along.

'I was there for the money. The mills were good to the workers and there were a lot of benefits. You could pack your job in in the morning and then get it back in the afternoon.

'We had a lot of laughs. We used to go to work with our curlers in beneath our headscarves. Someone would say, "Where are you going the night?" and the answer might be, "Nowhere, I've only got my curlers in to keep my headscarf on." And I mind sitting in the toilet, passing one fag between all of us.

'Nobody was a stranger. If you were a stranger to begin with, you soon got to know everybody, and they showed you the work. We all mucked in together, but you had to watch the pieceworkers, they behaved as if they thought you were taking away their livelihoods instead of everyone making their own piecework.

'The batches waiting to be done all had the machinist's number on them, and you got good batches and bad batches. Sometimes you didn't know it was a bad lot until it was on your machine and the threads broke. I used to wonder at first why some of the pieceworkers were going round looking at all the boxes. I didn't realise they were looking for the good batches for themselves, until a lassie told me when we were having a fag. Then I realised how some of them managed to be sitting there reading a book with their machines running like clockwork while I was going ten to the dozen, with my arms aching at the end of the day!'

Winners of the Ambulance Department Competition J. Clark-Neill Challenge Cup in 1910.
Photo Courtesy of the Old Paisley Society.

A Backbreaking Job

Sadie enjoyed the nights out, and the Christmas dinners at the Dallearn House Hotel in Barrhead, but the work became more difficult when she was on the twilight shift, and moved to Number 2 Mill after Number 1 Mill shut down,.

'In Number 1 Mill we stood at the machines, but in the other mill we had to sit on wheeled 'bogies'. The spools were in at the side of it, and we had to sit there the full shift, from 5p.m. until 11p.m. If you got up from your seat the ends of the thread broke, so if we wanted to go to the toilet we had to wait until they found someone else to take our place on the bogie.

'We were working with four reels of cones instead of the three reels we had before, and the bogies were on the same level as the cones, so that meant having to stretch forward to reach the furthest cones. It was a real backbreaking job. Sometimes when you got up at the end of the shift you could hardly move your back or your shoulders.

'It was good money, but after six months I decided that enough was enough and I left the mill and went to work in the schools. I preferred getting up at 5 in the morning to go to the school, to sitting at those machines.'

 # Moira (McFadden) Corrigan

Moira McFadden applied for a job in the Anchor Mill in the 1960s because 'I needed the money.' Her mother had worked in the Spooling Department in 1941, and her sister worked for many years in both Ferguslie and Anchor. 'She loved it, but I didn't.'

She was sent to the PA Winding Department on the 2nd floor. 'We were working with nylon wool, and I just didn't enjoy working there right from the start. Every time I stopped the machine to go to the toilet the forewoman was at my back. Believe it or not, I was the only one working on that floor that didn't smoke. The rest of them nipped out to the toilets for a smoke, but I kept getting into bother for going for the proper reason!

'The supervisor was a real slave driver, and I didn't like her. But several years later I met her again and I discovered then that I liked her. In fact, we became friends, and she was really surprised when I told her that I had detested her when I was in the mill.'

Moira stuck the job for nine weeks, then left. 'It just wasn't worth the hassle as far as I was concerned. But I kept in touch with some of the girls I met there, like Grace Phillips, who lived near me, and Sandra Neil. And, of course, the supervisor who turned out to be nice after all.'

 # Alex Higgins

Alex Higgins was never directly employed by the mills, but he played an important part in ensuring the comfort of mill workers. Alex was born in Orchard Street and the family later moved to Dunn Street. 'In Dunn Street we had a white sink and an inside toilet, which was very posh.'

His father was a brass finisher, and his mother and her sister had both worked in the Mills.

'My Aunt Mary had tuberculosis, and I remember being taken to visit her every week in the Sanatorium the Coats family had built at the Peasweep for their workers. She always looked so well, but each time she came home for a visit she began to look ill again after a week or two. When the

Sanatorium closed in 1948 the patients went to other hospitals, but Aunt Mary asked to go home. She died three years later.'

Milk Delivery Boy

While still a pupil at Williamsburgh School Alex became a milk delivery boy for Dales Dairy in Crossflat Crescent. The Anchor Mill was on his round. 'Wilson's of Johnstone, the carriers, delivered the big ten-gallon churns of milk to the mill canteen in the morning, and after school I took a two-wheeled bogey along there to collect the empty churns. The manageress then was a Miss Grant.'

On leaving school in 1938 Alex worked as a message boy for a butcher until he reached the age of 16 and became apprenticed to Pattison the plumber in Thread Street. 'My first job was to take bundles of copper pipe from Paisley to Linwood on a two-wheeled bogey. It was quite a struggle - there were about four bundles, each made up of six lengths of pipe, 21 feet long. Because the pipes were longer than the bogey they bounced, and my arms were continually bouncing along with them while my boots skidded and sparked over the causeys. By the time I reached the Linwood Road the sun was out, so then I kept getting stuck in the melting tar.

'We didn't have our own transport in those days, and everything had to be carried. I mind taking the tramcar out to Hawkhead once with a toilet pan under one arm, a blowlamp under the other, the toilet seat looped round my neck, and a bag of tools to carry as well!

'One of the journeymen I worked with at Pattison's was Norrie Rowand, a lovely man and a great worker. I still keep in touch with his son David, who is very keen on local history.'

'Coats Insisted on the Best'

Then Pattison's was sub-contracted to install footbaths in the Atlantic and Pacific Mills for the 'toe typists' - the women who worked barefoot so that they could use their big toes to switch their machines on and off.

'The materials we worked with were beautiful,' Alex recalls. 'That was the first time I ever saw a soap dispenser set in the wall. They are common now, but at that time they were a rarity.

'After that we were contracted to work on the toilets at the Mile End Mill. The plumbing system there was excellent. The toilets were walled with Vitrolite, a green glass material that looked like marble, and all the piping was hidden from sight. The mill lassies used to say that they had better toilets than the ones at Gleneagles Hotel! Coats insisted on the best for their employees.

'In those days the mill workers weren't allowed to bring cars onto the premises; only managers could drive to their work. Mr Leonard was in charge of the grounds at the Anchor Mills then, and played the pipes in the Mill Band. And there was Mr King, the Clerk of Works - he was very particular about the way things were done.

Fur Coat Ambitions

'I remember the mill girls coming out after a shift, "cleeking" arms and talking and laughing. And I remember as a child, seeing an older lady who lived in Thread Street who wore a plain shawl, one of the last shawls, I suppose, on her way to her work in the mill.

'A mill worker's dream, especially if she was an older, maiden lady, was to own a fur coat.'

Alex also did plumbing work in the homes of several mill managers and directors, as

Staff of Tube Winding, 5th Flat, Anchor's Mile End Mill on a night out. (Note the fur coats)
Photo Courtesy of Old Paisley Society

68

well as in houses owned by members of the Coats family.

In 1953, with a young family to support, he left Pattison's and went to work in the Glasgow shipyards, finishing his working career as a model maker for Babcock. 'That was a lovely place to work.'

Always a man who likes to be busy, he has spent his retirement learning different skills such as working with stained glass, and with wood. A true son of one of Scotland's most famous textile towns, he built a working spinning wheel that has been used by his wife Christina, herself deeply interested in all forms of textiles.

A keen fisherman, Alex well remembers the days when the Espedair Burn ran into Paisley green one minute and black the next because of all the dye works and mills built along its banks. 'But when they began to close down, the water started to run clear again. Fifteen years ago I caught my first salmon in the River Cart, at the Hammills, and now the river is home to sea trout and salmon.'

𝒫 Ian Clark (Seedhill Finishing Company) *𝒫*

After leaving Camphill School in 1949 at the age of 15, Ian Clark went into the Seedhill Finishing Company's laboratory. 'My sister was a secretary with the company and I wanted to go into the laboratory because I was interested in chemistry. We worked on sample dye patches to ensure the correct depth of the colours.

'The boss used to work away sometimes in a corner on his own. At first we thought that he was working on a special job but eventually it turned out that he was boiling and starching his handkerchiefs. He was known as TJ, and he was tall and long-limbed. Once when he found one of the students involved in a high-kicking competition with an employee he joined in - and won.'

Homers

In their spare time the laboratory workers did "homers", dying shirts, blouses, etc. 'There was always a pot boiling somewhere and sometimes mistakes were made. One man tried to dye a nice pair of his wife's kid gloves, a job that required a very low temperature. While he was on his tea break someone turned the temperature up and as a result the gloves turned out like hard prunes. Another chap tried to dye his girl friend's pale blue twin set but again, the temperature was too high and the sweater and cardigan came out doll-sized. The girl forgave him on condition that he dyed hanks of wool so that she could knit herself a new twin set.

'He set the temperature too high again and the hanks shrunk until they were like balls. That romance ended.'

Vyella and Clydella

Ian himself tried to waterproof his three children's duffel coats, but the temperature was too high and the leather toggles fell off. Then there was the time he left the boss's khaki lab coat unattended for five minutes when he was supposed to wash it. A prankster tipped a packet of orange dye into the water and Ian had a terrible time trying to restore the coat to its proper colour.

As well as working with a variety of materials including silks, satins and brocades, the Seedhill Finishing Company dyed and finished all the Vyella and Clydella for the entire country. 'Vyella and Clydella were spun in Nottingham, woven in Bridgeton, and finished and dyed in Paisley. We had a dying and printing works at Arkleston. We were also contracted to work with material for the Royal Air Force and the Army. The khaki material was always like sandpaper, even after it was finished, but the Air Force blue was of good quality.'

While working at the laboratory Ian attended night school at Paisley Technical College. 'I had been in the laboratory for about 18 months when the Works Manager walked into the laboratory and said, "I want you, laddie." I wondered what I had done wrong but it turned out that he wanted to train up an assistant - or, to be precise, he needed a "gofer". It was part of my job to hunt them down when the manager wanted to see them. In those days there was no tannoy, and although the factory was not large everyone had their special hidey-holes where they could nip off for a break or even to get a haircut.

Fly Smokers

'Anyone caught smoking was suspended for three days without pay. The dye-houses were filled with steam for a lot of the time and nobody could see a thing through it, so the folk who worked there could manage a fly smoke. The manager could smell the pipe or tobacco smoke, though, and he kept pouncing, in search of the culprits.

'Some who were caught and suspended worked out their own form of reprisal: when they heard the manager's voice through the steam they would fill a bucket with water and creep towards him. Then when they got within range they threw the water and retreated. He could never see who had done it.'

Eventually Ian was put in charge of the order forms from all over the country. Before work was done on the cloth it all had to be thoroughly checked to make sure that it was given proper treatment. 'We set up a musical group in that department, and the people above used to knock on the ceiling when we got too loud. We knocked back with cardboard tubes.'

The Problem with Smog

Later he moved to the sample department, where samples of all the cloth that came in from customers were laid on long wooden tables to be checked before work began on it. 'The works manager could never leave it to us - he always had to check it out himself, until the day he was running some cloth through his hands and a large skelf caught in the cloth went right into his finger. I had to use a penknife to get it out, and after that he left the checking to us.'

Ian ended his time with Seedhill Finishing in a department where he worked solely with Vyella and Clydella. 'There were only the two of us, my boss George Murray and me. They used to call us Clark and Murray, after a popular comedy stage act of the time. Smog was a problem as far as the Vyella was concerned. Even though it didn't get into the factory itself, it managed to leave large shadowy patches on the material. Nothing moved them - the only answer was to dye the cloth a darker colour to absorb the patches.'

After 22 years at the Seedhill Finishing Company Ian moved to another firm outwith Paisley. 'I felt that I wasn't going to move on much further by then, but I enjoyed my time at that factory. They were a good crowd to work with.'

 # The Hillington Weavers

(Margaret Brown, Dolly Matheson, Margaret Burns and Lisa Docherty)

Blackwood Morton, Kilmarnock - BMK - was one of the largest carpet manufacturers in the country, but their Hillington factory produced towels - hand towels, face towels and face cloths, bath sheets, and dishtowels.

'They made brilliant dishtowels,' says **Margaret Brown**, a weaver at Hillington for just over 40 years. 'Their goods were of top quality, but because of that they took longer to weave. What closed the factory in the end was that everyone started to buy imported, cheaper towels.'

When Margaret started work in the factory it was operating under the name of the Scottish Towel Company. She went there straight from school. 'The girl who lived up the stairs from us worked there and she said that it was a good job, so I applied.'

That was in 1958, and Margaret went into the Cellophane Department. 'We made up sets of towels, wrapped them in cellophane, and then used small heated irons to seal the cellophane. After six months there, I was moved to the weaving shed. I worked there for several years, then left when I was expecting my first child.'

Coping with Job and Family

While her children were young, Margaret returned to the weaving shed to work the 'twilight shift'. 'This meant that I worked hours that fitted in with having to see to the children. Then I went onto part-time, and got back to full time when my family was older.'

Like Margaret, **Dolly Matheson** had to fit work around the demands of a young family. Dolly, born and raised on the Isle of Lewis, came from a home where handloom weaving was part of everyday life. Her father owned a handloom.

When her children were young, Dolly, with an eye to getting back to work eventually, took a typing and shorthand course - then ended up in the BMK weaving shed at Hillington, where she discovered that there was a big difference between a domestic handloom and a factory weaving shed with fifty mechanised looms thundering away all day.

'I took on the job because the hours suited me. We stopped at 4 p.m. every weekday, and we had Saturdays off. This meant that I got home around the same time as

Santa and the staff of Anchor Mills Canteen preparing for a children's Christmas Party
Photo Courtesy of Old Paisley Society

the children, and had weekends at home. When I first started I planned to find other work once the children became more independent, but as it turned out, I stayed in that weaving shed for 30 years.

'I enjoyed my job. We had a good crowd in the weaving shed, they were more like family than workmates. When you were having a bad day, who else would you tell your troubles to but the folk you worked beside? We all had the same sort of worries - money, health, problems with the kids, falling out with our menfolk; we sympathised with the others when something went wrong, and we were happy for them during the good times.'

In the 1980s BMK closed the factory, by then known as Cooke's Sons, and it was taken over by Hadidas.

Back to the Weaving Shed

'The workforce was made redundant,' Margaret said, 'but Dolly and I were told when the job finished on the Tuesday afternoon that if we happened to be passing on the following morning at about 8.30 a.m., it might be worth looking in to ask about the chances of being taken on by the new company. So we did.'

'They asked us if, as well as weaving, we would be willing to take on whatever jobs that needed doing until things got back to normal,' Dolly recalls. 'And of course, we agreed to that, so we were taken on.'

For the first two months the factory was run by a reduced staff of about ten people, including management and office staff. During that time Margaret and Dolly were the only two weavers in the shed, and they also worked elsewhere in the factory when needed. 'We did whatever we had to do to keep the place going,' Margaret said. 'Hadidas was a good company to work for, they kept the factory going for ten years.'

'One of the bosses came back too, and he made the tea and did a bit of cleaning and manned the phones, so that Margaret and I could concentrate on working the looms and filling the orders,' explained Dolly.

Lisa Docherty first started in the Hillington factory as a machinist, hemming towels. 'I didn't want to go into the weaving shop because as far as I was concerned, it was far too noisy and I had no intention of working there. Then a friend who wanted to move into that department started trying to persuade me to go with her. I finally agreed to give it a try, and I discovered that once you got used to the noise it wasn't so bad, so I stayed.'

Sign Language

Lisa recalls that at one time the weaving shed floor had to be reinforced to support a new, modern type of loom the company wanted to install. 'The men were drilling, and the noise was terrible. We hated it - and then we discovered that the workmen hated the noise of the looms, and they were wondering how we could bear to work there every day!'

Like the machinists in the Paisley thread mills, the Hillington weavers communicated mainly by using their own version of sign language. Once new health and safety regulations came in they were required to wear earplugs at work, but even before then, Dolly always wore earmuffs because she knew that the noisy machinery could cause deafness.

When **Margaret Burns** first went to work at the factory she was based in the canteen, making tea and doing the cleaning. She then went into the Winding Department, and when a vacancy opened up in the weaving shed some of the weavers, knowing that she would fit into their 'happy band', persuaded her to apply. She did so, and got the job.

'We all got a production bonus and a quality bonus,' she explained. 'Every piece of work that came off the looms had to be checked, and if a batch was found to be sub-standard, the weaver lost out on her bonuses. Sometimes the boss would get into a temper when he found sub-standard work, and then the towels would be tossed into the air. If anything was wrong, it was always the weaver's fault.'

As happened in the Anchor and Ferguslie mills complexes in Paisley, the Hillington weavers had a love/hate relationship with the tenters, the men whose task it was to set up the looms, and deal with any breakdowns. The weavers were on piecework, and if a machine lay idle for any length of time, either waiting for the tenter, or taking a while to repair, the weaver lost out on her wages.

The Final Redundancy

Each weaver looked after at least four looms, and a fully experienced weaver could cope with six machines. At first there were male weavers as well as female, but when equal pay came in the men were gradually moved to other, better paid jobs.

As time passed, the number of working looms in the weaving shed was cut to twenty and the factory, trading by then under the name of Thistletex Towels, finally closed for good in March 2001, with all the workers being made redundant.

A few months later, Margaret Brown happened to be in Hillington, and discovered that the machinery was being dismantled. 'I went back for a last look round, and took some photographs. It was sad, seeing the weaving shed being emptied and the canteen being stripped. I have a photograph of the canteen table where we always sat during our breaks. We had some good times in that factory.'